I recommend "INTEGRATION, Heal Past Trauma and Prevent Future Trauma" for everyone searching for balance, health and reaching their highest potential. In these pages unfold the paths to self-reflection that lead to revelations. Integrating these revelations opens our inner guidance in each moment.

Mary Morrissey, Author and Founder of Life Mastery Institute.

"LET THE LIGHT FROM INSIDE BE YOUR GUIDE"

Workshops:
Moving Into Happiness
Maintenance for Optimum Health
It's Not About Money (Abundance)
Reunion & Rejuvenation (Pineal Gland Activation)
And many more

Lectures:
Reality 101 – The Grand Illusion
The Truth About Aging
Seven Steps to Manifestation
The Physical Body as Transformer of Chaos to Order
And many more

Radio Show Interviews with:
Caroline Myss
Drunvalo Melchizedek
Gregg Braden
James Redfield
Patricia Cota-Robles
And many more

Movies:
The Crystal Skulls Speak
Reflections

INTEGRATION

Heal Past Trauma and
Prevent Future Trauma

Shirley Rose, Ms. D.

Because of the dynamic nature of the Internet, any web addresses or
links contained in this book may have changed since publication and
may no longer be valid. The views expressed in this work are solely those
of the author and do not necessarily reflect the views of the publisher,
and the publisher hereby disclaims any responsibility for them.

The author of this book does not dispense medical advice or prescribe the use
of any technique as a form of treatment for physical, emotional, or medical
problems without the advice of a physician, either directly or indirectly. The
intent of the author is only to offer information of a general nature to help you
in your quest for emotional and spiritual well-being. In the event you use any
of the information in this book for yourself, which is your constitutional right,
the author and the publisher assume no responsibility for your actions.

Any people depicted in stock imagery provided by Getty Images are models,
and such images are being used for illustrative purposes only. Certain stock
imagery © Getty Images.

Second Edition August 2019

ISBN: 978-0-9636347-3-3 (paperback sc)
ISBN: 978-0-9636347-4-0 (eBook)

Integration:

Integration is the process of training ourselves to learn our life lessons in real time as they are happening to us.

Grab your pen and join me on a journey of self-discovery.

Special Thanks To:

Gloria Rubin for her critical eye.
Shanda Trofe from Transcendent Publishing
for the beautiful cover artwork.
Kathleen Black for her special drawings
inside the book.
Nancy Cain for her photo of me on the back cover.
Mary Morrissey for her thoughtful recommendation.

Share This with A Friend

If what we discover together moves you,
share this book with a friend.

10% of the Author's profits will be donated to:

Abe's House Corporation
(www.AbesHouse.org)
A Home For The Homeless

An organization
that provides housing for
the homeless.

Physical and Mental illnesses need to be treated. Listening to the small voice inside can lead us to the best treatments for us. Exploring traumatic experiences in our lives can help us heal emotional scars, that cause us to repeat patterns in our lives, that may not be for our highest good.

Healthy lifestyle choices are important for optimum health. Every choice we make affects us on many levels.

This book explores bringing greater awareness to our traumatic past, so we can see improvements in our outer world in relationships, work, finances and general wellbeing today.

Toxins in our air, water, food, skin care products, dental work, clothing, household cleansers, furniture, flooring, home building materials, exposure to radiation, smoking, drinking alcohol, drugs, stress, genetic predispositions as well as other factors also contribute to disease.

Contents

Introduction

My name is Shirley Rose. I studied Genetics in my undergraduate work in college and have a Doctor of Metaphysics. I bridge Science and Spirit.

Through my own personal experiences, I began to notice patterns in my life. I became aware that I was bringing the same kinds of relationships into my life over and over again. I was making poor choices in many areas of my life, and I wanted to change.

One day I had a revelation. Other people were expressing my anger for me. I was not expressing my own anger. As a result, I was bringing angry people into my life. In this Ah Ha moment my life changed.

I started exploring why I was angry. Where it all began for me? Little by little a story emerged, about my family and my past.

I started to take responsibility for my own feelings and understanding where my feelings came from.

I found myself INTEGRATING the original experiences in my life, that led me to this point. I let go of old patterns, and my life changed.

I am writing this book to share these experiences with all of you, so you can experience these life changing INTEGRATIONS for yourself.

And So It Begins

Chapter 1

Light was emanating through the window. The movement of the air touched my body gently. The heat from the overhead lamps were radiating all around me. Then suddenly and without warning I was upside down. SMACK. I was hit on my behind. SMACK again. My throat unleashed a wailing sound, primal and full. I was snatched away by two arms that drew me close to her body and moisture was siphoned from my nose.

"Where am I?"

"What am I doing here?"

I tried to squirm out of these strong arms that held me so tight. Soon I was bound in a blanket so firmly that no movement was possible.

"Who are these people?"

"What do they want with me?

I was handed to a woman lying in a bed. She was covered with sweat. I looked into her eyes and I knew. She was the one. The one I would travel through this life with.

I heard a voice,

"Let me hold her."

Two strange hands reached out, took me and held me right in front of his face. His stare was daunting, dark and mysterious. He seemed to be thinking, trying to penetrate through my eyes into my soul.

"He will be important to me too."

Then my eyes closed, and I fell into a deep sleep, a sleep that took many years to awake from. A forgetful sleep that left me wondering,

"What is going on here?"

Now I am older, looking back at life from the other end.

I am seeing patterns that eluded me in my younger years.

I am ready to wake up.

"Will you join me on this journey?"

The Great Escape

I was running, throwing off my clothes as I ran.

"I don't want to be confined."

My mother was chasing after me and picking up my clothes as I found my way across the street.

"STOP, STOP," she shouted.

"STOP."

I turned momentarily and smiled mischievously then scurried on faster than before.

Once she finally caught up with me there was yelling and laughing.

"Was she angry or amused?"

"You can't go around taking your clothes off?"

"Why not?"

"Because it is just not done."

I didn't really understand what she was trying to tell me. At two years old, I saw the world as a wide-open space for me to soar through at any speed I chose.

"Why can't I fly like I do in the higher realms?"

I felt confined again. Like when I was in a swaddling cloth.

And so, it began.

Limitation.

Socially Acceptable Behavior.

Being Less Than I AM.

Do you remember your first defining moment, the first time someone scolded you for being you? (Write about that memory here.)

That night in my sleep I floated over oceans, and reached up to the stars, and sat on distant planets, and played with wispy light beings that did not hold me back. They let me create the largest me I could be. And I was back HOME.

I did not want to open my eyes and rejoin the strange world below.

"Who made all these rules?"

With each passing birthday there were more rules, limitations, confinement.

I remember disapproving stares and explosive yelling. It wasn't directed at me, but I saw how my siblings were being treated when they did something "wrong".

"I will be good."

"I won't give my mother any reason to yell at me like that."

And so, I tiptoed my way through life.

I was the easy child.

I didn't do bad things.

I got good grades at school.

I did not make waves.

I avoided conflict at every turn.

I lost myself in dancing and singing, acting and playing, creating a world inside myself that was safe and fun.

I could go where ever my imagination took me and looked forward to sleep at night. I never had to be told to go to bed twice.

In my dreams, there were places of wonder and learning that were more fantastic than my waking life.

Extreme Controlling

And then I got married. I was eighteen years old. One month past my eighteenth birthday, that everyone seemed to ignore, because there was a Wedding to plan.

My husband was so filled with fear. His goal was to lock me up and keep me away from the people, places and things that I loved, so he could control me.

He would not give me a key to our apartment, because he never wanted me to come and go as I pleased. He would not let us have a telephone, because he did not want our parents to interfere with our relationship.

More rules, more confinement, more limitations.

"I am so confused and bewildered."

"Why does this man want to control me?"

Avoid conflict. Be the good wife.

We worked in his business and were together 24 hours a day.

Once a week I would stay home and clean. With no key, I left the door unlocked and walked down to the store to get the cleaning supplies that I needed.

He would not allow me to go to college.

Why didn't I leave then? Why did I stay?

I remember my siblings talking about how controlling our mother was. I never noticed. Remember, I was the good child. I never felt my mother's manipulations were aimed at me or were they.

"You must get married."

From the time I was small this message was pounded into me over and over.

So, was my decision to marry my own? Or was it what was expected of me?

Can you think of times in your life when you did something that made you unhappy? A situation you got yourself into and took a long time to get out of, or a situation you are still in? (Write about these times here.)

Sixteen years, two children and a lot of sadness later, I divorced my husband. I never regretted my choice to marry him.

He taught me independence; he was never there for me.

He taught me business; we ran a business together, which prepared me to get good paying jobs.

He toughened me up to life's difficulties and taught me how to work through things on my own.

He gave me two beautiful children and the means to give them a good life, which I enjoyed.

He showed me how anything was possible in the physical world. He was an amazing manifester.

He helped me to know that I did not want to be controlled ever again.

I guess I did not learn this from my mother, so Consciousness gave me a more extreme experience to Integrate this lesson.

Now he has passed away. I think that after people die, we think of them a little more fondly. We focus on remembering the good things.

He made me a strong person, able to accomplish anything I want.

Would I have learned this without him?

I suppose Consciousness would have found another way to teach me this.

But this is the way I chose.

I look fondly on my greatest teachers.

I can see that everything had a timeline in my life and that it all unfolded exactly as it was meant to.

Can you see the people that have been most challenging to you as your greatest teachers?

While still married, I began to follow a strict diet and exercise program. I was very disciplined.

"The Apple Diet," my friend Joan recommended.

She got it from her chiropractor.

One weekend per month, I would eat only apples: raw apples, apple sauce (homemade with no sugar) and baked apples. The rest of the month, I followed the "Fit For Life" diet from a leading book of the time on nutrition.

Being a busy mother, I exercised at home. I found a yoga class on PBS TV led by Richard Hittleman. For twenty minutes every day, I turned on the TV and followed his lead. I stood on my head and did all the postures, breathing and meditating.

I was experiencing great personal revelations from these practices of diet and yoga, which led to explosions of insights that began to guide me in a very deliberate way.

The small voice inside guided me to travel to faraway places, where I had profound spiritual experiences. I traveled to The Yucatan, Greece, India, the Four Corners area of the U.S., England, Scotland, Wales and Tibet to name a few.

I was guided to leave my marriage.

My Aching Back

The day my husband and I agreed to get a divorce, I went out into our garden and began to remove small wood chips from our flower beds.

I was angry at our gardener for not removing all the wood chips, so I decided to do it myself. I filled a large trash bag with the wood chips, lifted the bag, and twisted to move in the direction of the trash can.

I heard a loud Pop, Pop, Pop.

My whole back went out from top to bottom. I dropped to my knees.

I was home alone. I crawled into my house and got into bed. I could not move for three weeks.

I was paralyzed with fear at the idea of moving out into the world.

Eventually, I got help from a chiropractor.

But then something strange began to happen.

The Itsy-Bitsy Spider

From the time I was a child, I had a fear of spiders. My mother told me I was in the bath tub one day and was shrieking at the top of my lungs. She came running in and there on the wall was the tiniest, teeniest little spider you could ever imagine.

I remember how it felt when I saw a spider. I could feel the adrenalin rush that moved through my body. When a spider was standing still I was fine. But the minute it started running, I literally went into a fight or flight reaction.

My body went crazy, and I couldn't control it.

It was a phobia when I was a little girl that got better as I grew up, but I never really liked spiders.

One day about two months before I left my husband, I saw a spider on the bathroom floor. I stepped on it, and out came hundreds of baby spiders.

I continued to stomp on and kill every one of them.

Well, I was devastated. As a parent of two young children, I felt like a murderer.

In that moment, I decided to stop killing spiders.

But there was one problem, I could not live with spiders in my house. So, I created a devise to deal with this.

I went into the kitchen and got two paper cups. I gently moved the spider into one of the cups and quickly capped the first cup with the second cup. God forbid the spider should touch my finger or crawl out of the cup.

Then I took the spider outside and set it free.

> "You have every right to live, as long as it's not in my house."

Well, Consciousness began to test me.

The spiders started to get bigger and bigger.

One day, on the wall of my bedroom, where I slept at night, was the monster spider of all time. I am not exaggerating the spider was the size of my fist.

I looked up to God and said out loud,

"This is not fair."

"I am really scared!"

I knew that this was a test. I looked at the spider, and in my mind I thought,

"You know I could take my shoe off and smash you against the wall right now."

The spider did not move. I started to pace back and forth, and I wrestled with what to do?

"I know this is a test."

"I need to deal with this and move through my FEAR."

So, I went into the kitchen and got my two plastic cups. When I came back the spider was in the same spot, waiting for me.

I quickly put the spider in the cups and took it outside.

In that moment, I overcame FEAR. I Integrated FEAR. I realized that FEAR was a device that I created myself in my mind. It was not real. It was like those thin paper hoops that circus performers jump through.

Heal Past Trauma and Prevent Future Trauma

I jumped through the hoop. On the other side of the hoop, my fear was gone. I had conquered my fear. I would be able to face any fear that surfaced in my life.

Next, I promised myself that if I was ever afraid of doing something, I would make myself do what I was afraid of, so I could get over that fear.

Each time I faced my fear, I found that it got easier and easier.

Today spiders are one of my teachers. When they show up in my life, I look at them and must figure out what they have come to tell me. What fear am I dealing with?

Once I figure out what fear I am dealing with, I can take the spider out of the house. Sometimes I see small spiders and sometimes I see bigger spiders, but each time I must move through the barrier of my fear, jump through the hoop.

Have you ever felt paralyzed with FEAR?

How did you deal with it?

Can you think of any new ways you can deal with fear now?

On My Own

After my divorce, I moved and attended college. I studied Genetics. I felt my goal was to bridge Science and Spirit. During my studies, I found that each subject was saying the same thing using different words.

I remember writing up a laboratory experiment and thinking of it like an English paper. What was the purpose of the experiment? What did it mean?

A light bulb went off in my head and I saw how everything was connected English and Science and Archeology.

In Archeology, we thought about where things were found, what they were near, how they related to the people who left these artifacts. Everything was dependent on everything else.

I was seeing clearly now.

Perhaps one of the reasons I went to College was to see how all things are connected. To understand that people are speaking different languages, but they are all saying the same thing.

People were searching for meaning, for understanding, for purpose.

In that one moment, I Integrated that EVERYTHING IS ONE.

My worlds were colliding, and they would never be the same.

Have you ever found yourself attracted to specific practices or teachings?

Have you ever heard direction from the small voice inside that guided you on a new and unknown path?

For two years I focused on my classes and spiritual studies. Consciousness was supporting me every step of the way. I felt safe.

Holding My Ground

I signed up for a photography class that was a trip to the Yucatan. This class was taught by two teachers, a photography teacher, and a teacher who read the Mayan Hieroglyphs. I was interested in the Hieroglyphs.

A short time before we left, there was a huge hurricane in the Yucatan. Windows were blown out of hotels and there was wreckage everywhere. I was afraid to tell people I was going, because I knew they would try to talk me out of it. In my heart, I knew everything would be alright.

Most travelers cancelled their reservations, so that when our small group of nine entered Chichen Itza, we were practically alone. What an amazing gift. It was the same everywhere we went.

Hotels upgraded our rooms and we received wonderful service.

When I did mention to others that I was going to the Yucatan, they did try to talk me out of it. I did not allow their fears to affect me.

I have always felt protected. I know Consciousness is always watching over me. By following my inner voice, I had an amazing experience.

Expressing My Own Anger

I needed to hold my ground in other areas of my life too.

For most of my life, I kept my anger to myself. I wanted to avoid dealing with uncomfortable situations.

One day, I was having a shouting match with a friend.

Remember, my mother was a screamer too. I was trying to avoid my mother's wrath as a child, and now I was dealing with a similar situation that made me uncomfortable.

Right in the middle of this shouting match, I had this revelation:

> "She was expressing my anger for me, because I was not willing to express my anger myself!"

The minute I had this thought, she stopped yelling in the middle of a sentence. I had a revelation. I had Integrated this lesson, so I did not have to repeat it.

I noticed I was bringing angry people into my life, because I was not taking responsibility for my own anger. I did not want more angry people in my life! I decided that I would start expressing my own anger.

"What was I so angry about anyway?"

I was angry that my freedom was taken away from me. Was it taken away from me, or did I willingly give my freedom away to keep the peace?

I gave away my power to my mother, and now I was giving away my power to other people in my life.

I once asked my ex-husband, why men asked woman to compromise so much?

He said, "Because you let us."

I had to face up to the fact, that I let people control me. I let people confine me. I let people tell me what I could or could not do.

"No more."

"Never again."

I decided to live my life on my own terms. Not to be limited and made smaller than I AM.

I would dance, and sing, and travel, and find joy every day.

Have you ever found yourself angry?

What caused you to be angry?

As time went on, I got better and better at listening to my outside world for feedback of what was going on inside me.

I noticed and payed attention to the little things, like stubbing my toe.

"What was this pain trying to tell me?"

"What was pain after all?"

I realized pain was a messenger. It was my Subconscious Mind's way of communicating with my Conscious Mind, because my Conscious Mind was not getting the message.

I looked up every ache and pain in Louise Hay's book, "Heal Your Body." I explored the causes it suggested and searched inside myself to see if these were true for me.

I noticed that if I did not Integrate the lesson, something more drastic would happen to me. I would twist my ankle for example, which would take a longer time to heal. Or my back would go out which was very painful.

I decided to listen and understand pain.

And so, I began to listen. I found if I did Integrate the lesson in front of me, my body stayed healthy and strong. I suffered minor bruises, cuts and stubbed toes and immediately explored my anger and annoyance.

I did not let it escalate.

I got stronger and stronger, healthier and healthier.

"I was hooked."

I decided to begin a practice of paying very close attention to everyone I interacted with, to listen to what they were saying.

I knew it was my Subconscious Mind communicating with my Conscious Mind and I began learning the lessons as they were occurring.

I was INTEGRATING every day.

I realized that disease was caused by the amount of time it took for me to Integrate a painful experience in my life.

If I stubbed my toe and got the message, I could heal in a few days.

If I twisted my ankle and got the message, I would heal in a few weeks.

If I didn't listen and let it go for years, I could develop a life-threatening disease.

I consciously decided to choose Health.

Can you think of times when you suffered accidents or illness?

Can you go back to those times and remember what was going on in your life?

Were you angry, sad, depressed, worried or feeling trapped?

What could you learn from those experiences now?

Integration

Remaining Balanced and Healthy requires us to process our lives as we are living it. In this way we progress physically, emotionally, mentally and spiritually at the fastest rate possible.

We are evolving faster than ever before. It is so important to keep up with the reflections our experiences are teaching us.

In this way, we become our best selves and serve Consciousness in the most powerful ways.

Integration is the process of training ourselves to learn our life lessons in real time, as they are happening to us.

Disease is created by the length of time it takes, from the time we experience something traumatic, to the time we Integrate the lesson of this experience.

Noticing our experiences as they are happening and being fully present and aware of the lessons these experiences are teaching us, while they are happening, keeps us healthy.

If we do not get the lesson in our awareness, Consciousness will send us a signal. Sometimes these signals come in the form of physical pain.

Physical pain is a messenger, that signals we are not dealing with our emotional discomfort and the situations in our lives, that cause this discomfort.

If we stub our toe, and realize this pain is a signal that is trying to communicate some level of emotional discomfort in our lives. If we listen to what this pain is leading us to notice. Then the pain can stop right there, and we can Integrate the lesson.

If we refuse to listen, Consciousness will send us a stronger message. A situation that is even more stressful will come into our lives. A more painful physical condition will occur if we choose to ignore our lesson again.

This time we may fall and break our leg or twist an ankle. If we take the time to listen to what this pain is trying to communicate to us, and Integrate the lesson, then the pain can stop there. Now we don't have to keep repeating this traumatic experience. This pain has helped us Integrate this lesson.

If we still do not listen and ignore our trauma, years can pass. Then one day we may find ourselves being diagnosed with a life-threatening disease.

But we can still listen.

Even when we already have a disease, we can go deep inside ourselves and deal with the trauma we experienced as a child or adult.

Even at this late date, if we Integrate the lesson of these traumas, we can still heal.

The good news is that Integration happens in the moment of revelation. It is instantaneous. The moment the light bulb goes off in our conscious waking mind, the issue that caused the traumatic experience is resolved.

Our bodies begin to heal.

Now we do not have to repeat this lesson over and over again.

We can resolve to shift our consciousness one tiny notch, so we can create healthy habits in our lives from this day forward.

We can learn our lessons and have new experiences that are free of trauma.

We can do it consciously.

We can Integrate in every moment.

We can live joyous, peaceful, purposeful lives.

We are ready.

*The People
In Our Lives*

Chapter 2

Relationships with Our Parents or Primary Caregivers

As babies, we looked into the eyes of those holding us, singing to us, playing with us. We gave them our full trust. We trusted them with our lives.

Some of our caretakers got tired, angry, and were cruel. We were confused.

"What is happening here?"

"Is this the way it is supposed to be?"

We began to recoil.

"I don't like it when you do that to me."

"Something is wrong here."

Before we could speak, that place of inner knowing began forming opinions and reactions to everything happening to us.

When we were uncomfortable, we began to cry, or lash out, or throw tantrums.

We reacted to a stimulus.

Sometimes it was as subtle as the look someone gave us. Sometimes it was a response to a physical spanking or worse. Sometimes we were unable to get what we wanted or needed, like food or someone to change our diaper. Every day led us to trust our caretakers more or trust our caretakers less.

And so began our lifelong journey to heal from these experiences.

Losing Parts of Myself

I heard my mother screaming. She walked into my bedroom and sat down on my bed. She was out of control. At that moment, she was losing her mind, having a nervous breakdown.

Watching in disbelief, I found myself detaching. It was too hard to watch. Slowly I backed out of the room and closed the door. Eventually the screaming stopped. My mother walked out of my bedroom as if nothing had happened.

I was shaken to my very core.

"What had caused her to come to this?"

A part of me disassociated from myself. A part of me left my body because of what I saw.

I was bewildered.

I did not feel fear, I felt confusion.

Little by little over the years, more parts of myself left my body. It was my coping mechanism.

By the time I was in my late thirties, I began to suspect that more than 50% of my essence was now outside my body.

"I don't want to be here anymore."

I wanted to go HOME to that safe place I went when I was sleeping, that beautiful memory of the time before I incarnated in this lifetime. That place where I could create any desires instantly.

"Why do I have to stay here and be tortured?"

I had a child still living at home. I had responsibilities. I could not leave this world yet. But I wanted to.

Once I had the realization that it was my choice to stay in this world, my whole life changed.

I brought myself back into my body and began to experience myself and the world around me more fully. I was more present.

I could no longer blame other people for my circumstances.

I created my life here and now, just the way I created in my dreams.

If I created this, I could create something better.

And so, I began to watch my thoughts closely. Especially when I began feeling depressed.

A New Me

I started experimenting with new diets. I did many cleanses.

I would start over. I would clean out all the old negativity from my body and fill it up with better food, better thoughts, better choices, following through on ideas, and create the life I wanted.

I needed to get grounded and decided to find a job as a waitress. I would be serving others each day and finding joy and gratitude in my rewards.

I found myself comforting people, giving guidance and council, being a friend and confidant. I stopped focusing on my own problems.

Life started to get better. I was able to reach financial goals. I was bringing a better quality of people into my life. I was being appreciated. I began to flourish.

Little by little, I allowed myself small comforts, small enjoyments. It was okay to give something to myself. I did not only have to give to others.

I could take myself out to eat. I could give myself small gifts. I could make myself happy. What a revelation!

"I could make myself happy!"

This changed everything. I did not need other people to make me happy, to give me the things I wanted. I could give these things to myself.

I started doing more things I enjoyed. Life became worth living again.

Have you ever been in a dark place in your life?

Were you waiting for someone else to make it better?

What could you do today to make yourself smile?

Our perception played a large role in how much these experiences affected us.

Perhaps we misinterpreted the intention of someone, perhaps we did not understand what was happening to us, and we panicked.

It is possible that our interpretation of these events in our lives were made worse, by what we were feeling at the moment they occurred.

If we were tired, feeling weak, or depressed at the moment someone lashed out at us, we were not prepared to be strong.

By remembering what we were feeling, we can notice that in our moments of weakness, we were even more traumatized than we would have been if we were balanced.

After many experiences, I realized there is no right or wrong.

There is no good or bad.

There is no one to blame.

There is just trauma that accumulated in my physical, emotional, mental and spiritual bodies.

So much of this happened on an unconscious level.

So much of this was pushed down deep inside me.

I did not want to feel the pain that thinking about or understanding these experiences brought me.

I just did not want to deal with it.

Now we can all change that and look a little deeper.

Siblings and Playmates

Next brothers and sisters came into our lives. Friends and extended family members interacted with us. More looks, more ruff and tumbling, more falls, more confusion.

Coming into a world we do not understand, is a scary place to be. Now we do not just want our caretaker's attention, we are competing for it. We are competing for playthings, and playtime, with friends and siblings. We are beginning to feel the power struggle.

We do not always understand the rules.

"Wait your turn, share your toys, don't hit or bite."

The world is filled with socially acceptable responses and when we choose the "wrong one", according to our caretaker, there are consequences.

They are yelling at us. They are hitting us.

"What did we do wrong?"

It is not always clear. Maybe our caretaker had some bad news and is taking it out on us. Maybe they are tired, and just can't handle one more thing. And they just snapped.

So, what are we learning?

"People can be unpredictable."

It doesn't make any sense to us.

"We didn't do anything."

"Why is this happening?"

Life is getting more complex. We just do not understand.

Do you have struggles with your siblings today? Where did these struggles start?

Taking It Out on Someone Else

Over the years, I have had several friends who were the first born in their families.

Some of them told me how they resented having to look after their younger brothers and sisters.

They could not spend time with their friends or do the after-school activities they wanted to do, because they had to watch their siblings.

Sometimes these people got angry and resentful. And sometimes they took their anger out on their brothers and sisters.

They felt they were not able to be kids themselves. They were thrust into adulthood at an early age.

Sometimes these people took their anger out on people at school.

Bullying has become a big issue in today's world. Bullies are people who are expressing their pain in inappropriate ways.

We are all in some kind of pain. Showing kindness and compassion, and really listening to those who hurt us, can teach them by example to act in new ways.

Forgiveness changes everything. Telling those that have hurt us that we forgive them, can shift their entire perception.

Sending love and positive intentions to those who are suffering around us, can uplift everyone.

Lasting solutions to inappropriate behavior need love and compassion in a continuous stream.

People need to begin to trust again, before they can change their ways.

Trust is a slow process that is reinforced over long periods of time.

When people are exposed to kind and generous actions, over and over again, their beliefs about the world begin to change.

"I am worthy of love."

"There are kind people in the world."

"I am ready to create a better world for myself."

To make the world a better place, we need to do kind and generous acts every day.

We need to listen to the body language, and unspoken words of people around us, who are unable to express their pain in constructive ways.

We can bring compassion into the world in every moment.

Have you ever felt like you had to do things you didn't want to do?

Have those frustrations led you to treat the people around you in cruel ways?

Could you go inside now, and look at the experiences that caused these frustrations?

What could you do now, to Integrate the lessons of those experiences?

Starting School

We start school. More rules, more socially acceptable ideas. Maybe our ears stick out, and kids make fun of us. Maybe our teeth are crooked. The power struggle continues.

Children are now competing for the attention of teachers, friends, social status, popularity, and acceptance. There are bullies, and there are people who are so good at everything. We start to doubt ourselves. We start to judge ourselves, the way others are judging us.

And here we are interacting with people who are like our caretakers, and some that are different from our caretakers. But we notice, we feel more comfortable around people who are like our caretakers, even if our caretakers are cruel.

It is time to notice this.

It is time to pause and begin to see the patterns.

Following the Crowd

I met a new friend at school. She was more popular than my other friends. She told me to stop seeing one of my best friends and I did. I began to be more popular myself.

My mother got a call from my old friend's mother asking what happened? She didn't know of course, and I never explained.

Looking back, I now see how cruel that was. I felt very bad about it, and years later met my old friend again by chance. I reconciled my feelings about how I had treated her and felt that she forgave me.

We did not have all the insights and experience, when we were young. We all made choices that we look back on, and may regret, or think of other ways we could have handled these situations.

With time and experience, we gain deeper understanding of how other people feel. We may become more compassionate, and think of how we would feel if someone did these things to us?

What did I learn from this?

"We are all fragile."

"We all want to be accepted."

"Think before I act and imagine how it may affect the people around me."

Was there ever a time when you regretted your actions?

If you were in the same situation today, what could you do differently?

By Integrating our lessons, we can see more clearly and act on higher levels of Consciousness.

Boyfriends and Girlfriends

We begin to feel sensations in our bodies, when we are around certain people. We want to spend more time with them.

"Do they want to spend time with me?"

If those we are attracted to, don't feel the same, we feel rejected. We react to this rejection in many ways.

Perhaps our self-esteem suffers, perhaps we get angry, and perhaps we start bullying other people, because we are not getting what we want.

Or perhaps, we do things to other people that we saw our parents doing to each other.

Everything begins with our first impressions. The moment we are born, we begin to notice what is around us. All these sensations are adding to how we feel about our bodies and ourselves.

Were we rejected by our mother?

Did she refuse to hold us or nurse us?

Was our craving for closeness met, or did we find ourselves ignored and feeling neglected?

As we begin to have romantic relationships, all these feelings and emotions emerge.

For some of us, they are great impressions, and we attract affectionate and kind partners to us.

For others, our critical parents, siblings, friends and teachers, left their mark on our self-esteem. We drew partners into our lives who were critical, angry, and didn't give us what we needed or wanted.

Over and over again, the patterns circle around us. We keep attracting the same kind of people into our lives as our caregivers were.

My Ex-Husband Was Like My Parents

My ex-husband was like my mother because he was a screamer and like my father because he was a hustler in business.

My father died when I was young, so I did not really know him very well. He was often away on business.

When my mother was dying, her brother, my uncle, came to see her one last time before she passed. My uncle stayed with us for a while until after the funeral.

My uncle's son and my ex-husband also came for the funeral. My uncle and ex-husband got along really well. They were laughing and joking together. They were having a great time with each other.

My uncle and my father were very close. My father was like a second father to my uncle. They shared many important events in each other's lives. My father's death left a void in my uncle's life.

My uncle's son commented to me that he had never seen his father light up like he did with my ex-husband. That was the first time I realized how much my ex-husband was like my father.

I always knew he was like my mother, because of his screaming, but I did not know he was also like my father.

This indirect feedback from my cousin gave me a realization.

"I had chosen someone just like both my parents to marry."
What a shock!

I did this unconsciously, unaware of the fact that I felt attracted to people who were just like my parents.

This was the moment that my Conscious Mind got the message. I Integrated the lesson.

That marriage did not go well. I did not want to repeat this pattern in my life.

New Relationships

I found my voice.

With each new relationship my voice grew stronger.

I was able to express my feelings. I was also able to set limits, in behaviors I was not comfortable with.

I shared my hopes, and my fears with my boyfriends.

I allowed myself to be vulnerable and show my true self to the people I was close to.

I was always surprised that when I was honest with my boyfriends, they seemed to understand.

I was learning how to be in healthier relationships.

With each new relationship, I noticed that I was dealing with different issues, and resolving them.

Each relationship got better and better.

I brought a higher quality person into my life each time. I was receiving more of what I wanted to experience, with each new relationship.

I was loving myself more, and the world around me was reflecting that back to me.

There have been times in my life, when I now realize I over reacted to a situation.

Many of these times were triggered by feeling controlled.

I would flash back to my feelings in my early childhood, and marriage.

I was reacting to those times in my past, when I did not express my feelings.

In a way, my over reacting helped me to heal my past.

Once expressed, my anger disappeared. I was able to move on.

I can now look back at those times, grateful that I finally stood up for myself. This really empowered me, knowing that I could protect myself, made me feel safe.

I was able to change my old patterns, and act in new ways.

We can all begin to use new tools.

We can begin to examine our reactions, to things that do not make sense in the moment.

Did we over react to this present experience?

Could this be because, we were triggered to remember the time our parents, siblings, partners, or friends hurt us in this same way?

Can we break the cycle once and for all, by finally Integrating the lessons this pain is trying to bring into our Conscious Mind?

We can.

Can you remember a time, that you over reacted to what was happening to you?

Did this situation remind you of something from your past?

Workplace Managers and Fellow Workers

It is my first day at work. I am scared and nervous.

"Will I do the right things, say the right words,

understand all the new rules?"

Suddenly, we notice that our Supervisor is treating us just like our parents did. Fellow workers are making fun of us, just the way kids did at school. We are given projects we don't feel capable of being successful at. Just like we felt when we took that big test at school.

"What is happening?"

"Did we notice this?"

Or, are we just feeling sad, inadequate and rejected again. It is our choice.

Instead of repeating these same old patters, we can now choose to stop and take stock.

"Why do I feel bad about this?"

"When did I first feel like this?"

We can close our eyes, and play the movie in our mind, of the original situation that happened, when we were babies, children, and adults.

Feel how we felt then. Notice what lesson Consciousness was trying to help us learn?

What can we see?

Can you remember a time when you felt uncomfortable in a work situation?

What could you have communicated differently, to the people in your workplace, to help you feel more comfortable?

I once told a coworker, that I felt she was talking down to me when we spoke.

To my surprise, she thanked me and said, she had gotten this same comment, at other places she worked.

This broke the ice between us. We enjoyed each other's company after that.

When we take the time to communicate our feelings, in constructive ways using statement that start with I feel, people do not feel they are being blamed or attacked.

Would you want someone to approach you, if you were doing something that made them uncomfortable?

Feeling Controlled Again

I have been in jobs where I was given the freedom to work in my own way. In these positions, I thrived.

I was even given prizes and bonuses for the quality of my work.

In jobs where I felt micromanaged, I felt controlled.

Eventually, I began to feel resentful in these positions, and left.

This was progress, and I was grateful for that.

What was different, was how I reacted to feeling controlled. I was able to stand my own ground, give my opinions, voice my disagreements, and in the end, choose to change my circumstances.

I knew I was evolving and moving in the right direction.

We have come into this life to learn.

We learn by overcoming our fear.

Perhaps we are here, to go through our worst nightmares, so we can go through these experiences, and come out changed.

Perhaps, that is why we are experiencing so much unpleasantness.

Shifting our perception, to see our experiences as lessons and not just challenges, can take a lot of the drama out of our lives.

There are three kinds of learning:

- Wisdom: I needed to experience this to focus on my lesson.
- Understanding: Now I see why I brought that abusive person into my life.
- Integration: I forgive the person who hurt me, because now I realize, this person was only facilitating my need to have this experience.

Consciousness created this situation, to give me an opportunity to become stronger, and act in new ways.

Once we Integrate one lesson, we go on to learn the next lesson through experience.

If we do not Integrate this lesson now, we repeat the same lesson over again.

We are moving in a spiral up the ladder of evolution.

Healing

When we begin having these insights, we notice something strange.

Instead of having a romantic partner treat us abusively, someone at work is treating us badly. Then perhaps a friend treats us in a way we don't like. An acquaintance then does something we are uncomfortable with. Then a stranger may yell at us for no reason, on the street.

The pattern we have been experiencing begins to distance itself from us, step by step. When we first had this experience, it may have been with a parent, then a spouse, then a friend, then an acquaintance, then a stranger.

Slowly the pattern moves farther and farther away from us.

Next, instead of having people treat us abusively, we have a close friend come to us and tell us they are being treated the same way we were.

Then we notice situations where acquaintances are being treated like we were.

Next, we notice strangers in line at the movies and where we are shopping being treated that way.

Finally, we notice we have not seen this particular pattern moving around us for a while.

The old pattern is moving farther and farther away from us. We are letting go of the need to be treated in these old ways.

We can move on in our life in a new direction. We can draw people into our lives that treat us with greater respect.

We may find that the process reverses.

We notice a couple in line at the movies holding hands and being affectionate with each other.

We notice acquaintances in relationships we admire.

We hear stories from our friends that some wonderful new person has come into their lives.

And finally, we may start meeting people that treat us with kindness. People who appreciate us, and praise us, where we work, and then in romantic relationships.

We are now attracting new patterns because of our new beliefs.

"There are kind people in the world."

"I choose to be around kind people."

"Kind people are in my life."

Each issue is healed one at a time.

We may notice that with each new relationship, we are getting closer and closer to what we ultimately want, a whole and loving relationship of two people, who give and take with equal measure.

The process may take time, but the Integration of one issue can happen instantly at the moment of revelation.

Often the chain of events mentioned above is set in motion in a single second of conscious awareness.

- <u>Wisdom:</u> I did not feel deserving of kindness in my life.

- <u>Understanding:</u> I needed to transform this belief.

- <u>Integration:</u> I brought experiences and people into my life to help me shift.

I forgive myself for feeling this way. I forgive my parents, spouse, and friends, for treating me unkind. They were just helping me to grow. I now have more compassion for others and treat them more respectfully.

Can you remember a relationship that did not work out?

What lesson did you learn from this person?

Expectations

Recently I saw the play "Follies," with music and lyrics by Stephen Sondheim. As I walked out of the theater, I reflected on the relationships the play portrayed.

I had a revelation, Integration:

> "My expectations in relationships caused me a lot of disappointment and sadness."

Just as I am responsible for my own happiness,

> "I am also responsible for my own sadness."

> "Wow!"

All that blaming others for not doing what I wanted them to do, not saying what I wanted them to say.

"I created my own disappointments."

Perhaps it was my Ego who created those expectations, or society telling me what I should want.

"He doesn't call me often enough."

I felt neglected and unloved.

"He forgot my Birthday again, and our anniversary."

I felt unappreciated and sad.

On Valentine's Day he wasn't imaginative enough and just got me a card.

"Where is the romance?"

I felt left out and alone.

No one can live up to these kinds of fantasy expectations, and they know it. So many men don't even try. They do nothing, rather than doing the "wrong" thing.

We make ourselves miserable with fairy tale expectations in relationships.

The same is true for our expectations of our parents, partners, and pals.

We have unrealistic expectations for the perfect holiday meal, a great family vacation without conflicts, friends who will put up with our bad behavior, because they should accept us for who we are.

I realized:

> "No one and nothing outside of myself, can make me feel anything!"

> "I am responsible for all my own feelings!"

Imagine a life without expectations.

> "Wow!"

I Integrated that,

> "The secret to life is to enjoy THIS moment, as it is!"

By stringing together these moments I was creating a Joyful life.

Without expectations, the experiences I am having do not need to be compared to some imaginary fantasy.

> "I can appreciate what I have here and now."

I started to focus on all the wonderful experiences I was having every day.

I felt grateful for everything.

My life became a blessing and a Joy.

Would you like to choose Joy? What are you Joyful about in THIS moment?

What is Happening in Our Life Now

We can see how well we are doing by what is happening in our life right now.

"Thank you for opening that door for me."

"Thank you for holding that elevator for me."

"Thank you for letting me go in front of you in line because I only have one item."

Often small kind gestures, by friends and strangers, begin to happen.

People begin to smile at you. They sense a new light energy emanating from inside you.

"Thank you for giving me your seat on the bus because I am holding a lot of packages."

As we experience more kindness in our lives, new messages are being formed.

"People are kind."

"People can be trusted."

"People are there for me when I need them."

These new patterns are embedded deep inside our Subconscious Minds.

It is important to notice these new patterns, acknowledge them, and be aware of them. Move these patterns into our Conscious Mind and be Grateful for all the wonderful changes around us.

"I am deserving of abundance." "I am deserving of love."

"I am deserving of Joy."

Small shifts take hold, and we find ourselves smiling throughout our day for no reason.

Life is delightful and peaceful.

What kind gestures have people done for you recently?

What changes have you noticed in your life lately?

What changes would you like to see in your life now?

Emotions Emerge

Chapter 3

Emotions Are Reactions to Experiences

Emotions are energy in motion. Each feeling carries a unique energy signature. This energy moves through us and around us.

Emotions influence everything in our lives.

How we feel in the moment that something is happening to us, influences how we feel about that experience, as we reflect back on it.

If we are angry or unbalanced in that moment, we may mix these feelings with what is happening outside of ourselves.

We can transfer our anger to the people around us.

This transferred anger can trigger explosive actions in other people.

The feelings that come up, when we are having a traumatic experience, set in motion a series of events that can lead us to greater Health and Awareness, or to the beginnings of disease.

Just as we are taking in information from the moment we are conceived, we are also reacting to and interpreting those observations through feelings.

Every person reacts differently.

If many people are sharing the same experience, like being in a train crash, the internal processing of trauma will be different for each one of them.

Can you think of a traumatic experience in your life?

How were you feeling just before it happened, while it happened and after it happened?

Would you feel different about this experience now, if you were in a balanced state while it was happening?

Being in a balanced state, is when our thoughts, words and actions are all aligned with the same positive intention. Our physical, emotional, mental and spiritual bodies are nourished, content, clear, and inspired.

Our movements are consciously created.

The world around us reflects our wholeness through abundance in finances, family, friends, relationships and work that feeds our soul.

When we see chaos, from this point of view, it is experienced internally with greater understanding, and less reactivity emotionally.

We see these chaotic patterns, and acknowledge them as transient states, that will eventually come back into equilibrium.

Hormone fluctuations, candida overgrowth, parasites, heavy metals, and other toxins in our body, can make us feel emotionally unbalanced, as well as physically ill.

Doing cleanses regularly, may keep these toxins at manageable levels, which can help us sleep better, and have fewer cravings for foods that are not healthy for us.

Sitting quietly, and discovering the cause of our imbalances, can lead us to solutions.

Am I hungry? Did I sleep well last night? Did I drink a lot of alcohol or eat a lot of sugar last night?

Are you feeling balanced right now?

Our Innate Personality

We are born with an innate personality, that may tend toward being positive or pessimistic.

Some of this may be inherited, and some of this may be a part of who we are.

We have all met people, who constantly make lemonade out of lemons in their lives. These people seem to find the positive side of everything.

We have also met people, who find fault with everything and everyone around them. It is as if these people, have a filter in front of their eyes, that colors everything with darkness.

Whichever filter we were born with, we can slowly reprogram ourselves, to shift to a pattern, that moves us toward a Higher state of Awareness, and a greater level of health.

Emotions are the fuel that gives us energy. This energy can be used to make our lives peaceful and tranquil, or chaotic and filled with drama.

The emotions of the people around us, can also influence us and make us more afraid.

We can take on their emotions as our own. But we always have a choice.

If we begin to observe ourselves, and how the world and people around us are affecting us, we can start on a path that leads us to conscious living.

Conscious living is the process of Integrating Life in ways that lift us up, to see our lessons clearly.

We then process our lessons with insights. Life is our teacher.

Life is teaching us to be beings, that add Light to ourselves, and the world around us.

Each one of us is the Healer of ourselves, and our World.

Are we ready to make this shift, and work together to create the World we want to see every day?

We are!

What personality type are you?

Would you like to change that personality type? How could you do that?

Travel Angels

During my process of personal evolution, I was led to travel to many places around the globe. I am a person who likes to plan everything ahead of time. However, Consciousness had something else in store for me.

Once I arrived in another country without any reservations. It was my intention to join a tour when I got there. When I called the company I was interested in, they informed me that I could not make reservations from this country. This company only took reservations from the United States.

I remember hanging up the phone. My heart started pounding. I started breathing erratically. I was hyperventilating. I was having an anxiety attack.

"I have to slow down."

"I have to start breathing deeply."

Slowly I came back into balance. My body and mind began to relax.

"What to do next?"

I looked around and tried to think clearly. I would find a Travel Agency, of course.

"There has to be a Travel Agency somewhere in one of the biggest airports in the world."

"Where is the Travel Agency?"

I asked one of the people in uniform.

"No Travel Agency in this airport," I was told.

But I did not believe this. I felt there had to be one. So, I started roaming around, wandering down one way and then the next. Eventually I found a Travel Agency.

"Today is Sunday and this is the only Travel Agency open in the whole country."

I was so grateful. Soon I had reservations in a wonderful hotel.

"Take public transportation right here in the airport. It will take you all the way to your hotel."

I boarded the subway system.

Kind strangers helped me get my luggage on the Train.

When I got off at my stop a young woman helped me carry my many bags up the stairs.

I found myself across the street from my hotel.

She continued to help me carry my bags all the way into the hotel where a bellboy took my luggage to my room.

I started to call these helpers my Travel Angels. Without them I might have fallen into complete despair. Where ever I turned there were people to assist me.

During my travels, I found myself in a very large site. It was a huge site and very spread out. I was looking at the map given to me at the entrance, trying to figure out where I was, when a young man approached me.

> "I have lived here all my life. I will show you all the hidden places of this site."

And so, I followed over fences and up hills, I was being pushed to the limits of my endurance. I kept going.

When we arrived back at the entrance late that afternoon, I found I missed my bus back to my Bed and Breakfast.

I looked around and noticed many tours boarding people on their buses.

> "Would you please drop me off near my Bed and Breakfast? I missed my bus."

> "Sure."

And so, I hopped in sore and tired.

> "I won't be able to walk tomorrow after all this," I thought.

When I got back to my Bed and Breakfast, I took a long bath and then went to sleep. To my surprise, I felt fine the next day. The hot bath rejuvenated and relaxed my body.

On that same trip, I met a woman from America at a conference. We decided to do some traveling together. She had a guidebook of sights she wanted to visit.

One of her intended destinations was far away. She was flying there. I decided to take a train and meet her there.

As I was boarding the train, people were yelling to me:

> "There are no rooms. There is a rock band giving a concert there and all the rooms are booked up."

I smiled and waved goodbye. After everything I had been through, I knew Consciousness would find a way to take care of me.

While sitting on the train, I noticed a young woman with a child sitting across from me. Two men were harassing her, and she came over to me and asked if she could sit next to me.

"Of course."

We started chatting. I told her where I was going, and that I needed a place to stay. She stood up and made a call from her cell phone. When she came back:

"I have a place for you to stay. My friend is meeting us at the train station and you can stay with her."

I smiled. Here was another Travel Angel. I was getting used to this. I stayed at her friend's home and she showed me around the area taking hikes and visiting local spots.

She let me leave much of my luggage at her home, drove me to the bus station, and gave me a key to a place she owned, where I could spend the night before heading to my next destination.

By letting go of fear, and not listening to other people's fears about there not being any place to stay, I opened myself up to the assistance of Consciousness, which is always there for us.

Little by little throughout this trip, I learned to surrender.

I was able to give up my tendency to want to control everything. I relaxed into the process of trusting, that I would find my way to everywhere I needed to be.

I was traveling for about five months.

When I came home, I would have to make some decisions about the rest of my life.

I used my time on this trip to watch and learn.

Family Dynamics 101

Throughout the five months of my travels, I met many different families. I was able to spend a lot of time with them and was able to view their family dynamics at close range.

The children in these families were running their parent's lives.

It was interesting to notice, how their children dictated their lives, and how their relationships were impacted by their children's behavior.

I began to examine my own life deeper.

"What choices would I make when I got home?"

The experiences I was having on this trip were preparing me, to make choices that would uplift my life.

Since the day they were born, my children have always come first in my life.

I put myself last on my list.

I did not stay in touch with my own needs and dreams.

I began to be aware that my life was out of balance.

I had to start considering my own needs, as well as my children's needs.

Both were important.

Consciousness is very clever. It will teach us lessons and take us where we need to go, to observe situations that can prevent us from creating a future filled with challenges.

We can learn our lessons, by seeing how our lives would turn out, if we followed the paths these other families took.

I decided to take a different path and learn from what I was shown.

The first step is to be aware that what is happening around us is teaching us lessons.

The second step is to be aware of the lessons we are being taught.

The third step is to decide, if we want to continue a path that may lead us to sorrow and despair, or if we want to change the direction of our current path, to move toward a life of greater joy and fulfillment.

Life is made up of choices.

By Integrating the lessons of our life, we notice what is going on around us.

Then we decide, if we want to continue having these types of experiences.

Or, if we don't like what we see, do we want to move in a new direction to change our lives?

Can you think of any situations in your life, where Consciousness was showing you how your life might look, if you continued your present path?

Do you like the path you are on now?

If not, you can change that path.

Just start thinking about the life you would like, the job you would like, the relationship you would like, the home you would like to live in.

Today can be the start of something wonderful!

Taking on Our Parents Emotions

Emotions are the indicators. They tell us how we are feeling each step of the way?

Is what we are seeing in our outer world making us uncomfortable?

Have we become comfortable with abusive relationships, because these kinds of relationships are familiar to us?

Are we becoming our parents?

Are we taking on the judgements, and fears, of our parents?

Parents are constantly passing their judgements, and fears, to their children.

Everything our parents say to us is colored with the totality of their experiences, traumas, and fears.

We not only believe them, because they are the source of all our information about the world for many years, but we take on many of their attitudes, and phobias as well.

We copy what our parents do. That is how we learn.

These ideas, and fears, can be so ingrained in us, that we do not even realize that we are taking on their ideas, and fears.

We may be totally unaware that many of the challenges in our lives are not our issues. They are our parent's issues.

Watching my Mother Transition

I had the blessing of spending the last three months of my mother's life with her.

I moved her close, to be near me, and spent time with her every day. She was on morphine for pain. She had cancer.

I listened to her drug induced visions, that brought out her fears about things that happened in her life.

I saw her attitudes shift. She finally found peace. Then she was ready to transition.

If you have ever had the privilege of watching someone closely toward the end of their life, you may have noticed these things too.

As she told me the stories of the experiences she was having in her head, I reminded her that these thoughts and visions were not real.

"But they seem so real."

Isn't this true of life? Our outer experiences seem so real. We forget that everything that happens to us, on the outside, starts on the inside.

Our fears, our hopes, our desires, drive us to act and react in ways that shape our experiences.

As I watched my mother die, I began to realize that many of my issues were really her issues.

After she passed, I literally felt all her issues lift up and out of my body. These issues looked like white steam rising from my shoulders and head.

My body went into shock. After some time, I realized what had happened.

I was bringing experiences into my life, to work out not only my own issues, but my mother's issues too. Wow!

A huge burden was lifted from my shoulders. I no longer needed to carry those heavy bags with me.

A somewhat euphoric state set in, and I began to view the world around me differently.

The traumas of my mother's life had been removed. I was now seeing through my own eyes, maybe for the first time. Now everything looked different.

I felt differently about what I saw in the outer world. Our Emotions drive us in every possible way.

If we let our emotions rule us, we are subject to lives filled with drama.

If we understand that like pain, emotions are messengers, trying to make us aware of what is really going on inside us.

If we dig deeper inside ourselves, at times we are most emotional, we may find the root cause of our feelings.

We may remember the first time we felt like this, and what happened then?

Can you think of a time when you were very emotional, and it seemed like you were not reacting to what was happening in front of you?

Were you reacting to a trauma you experienced long ago, or last week?

Can you think of why Consciousness was showing you the same lesson again?

Are you ready to dig deeper, and figure out what you need to learn, so you don't have to keep repeating this lesson?

Watching Our Thoughts

It is just as important to address our emotional pain, as it is to deal with our physical pain, because our pain starts in our emotions.

"That person gave me a dirty look."

"They hurt my feelings."

Now we begin to feel bad about ourselves, because someone seemed to judge us harshly. We begin to believe,

"I am not good enough."

"There is something wrong with me."

These very thoughts start to create changes in our bodies, that start the process of disease.

We need to watch our thoughts every moment.

As soon as we hear a negative thought, we need to stop ourselves, and replace it with a positive thought.

Through time we can train ourselves, to have better thoughts.

"We are what we think."

We have heard this many times.

Choosing Joy

I was in a transitional moment in my life again. I sat down and thought:

"If I could do anything, what would I do?"

"Make movies."

When I was six years old, I found refuge in the movies.

At six, I was allowed to walk the very short block to the movie theater and buy a ticket. In those days you could pay once and watch the movie as many times as you liked.

Often there were double features, two movies playing.

In the evening, my mother would come to the movie theater to get me for dinner.

The screen looked enormous to me, and I found myself lost in the world inside it.

It seemed real to me, this other world on the movie screen, like the world inside me.

This began a lifelong love of the movies.

So, what could be better than to make my own movies? I went to my computer and printed a card:

"Shirley Rose – Independent Film Maker."

Shortly after that, a friend of mine called, and asked if she could come and stay at my house for a couple of days.

I said "Sure."

While she was at my house, she got a call asking her to be in a movie. She said she wasn't interested in doing it, but that the contact might be a good one for me.

I was open for anything.

Soon I was in Los Angeles, touring a production studio through her contact.

I also visited a group and announced that I was making a movie, and if anyone was interested in joining me on the project, to let me know.

I went on vacation and forgot all about it.

When I returned, there was an e-mail from someone who wanted me to make a film about Crystal Skulls. She had recently acquired one and shared her story with me.

I said "OK."

I went to her apartment and started shooting a film about her and her crystal skull. She also invited two other crystal skull owners. I interviewed them all.

A while later, an old friend showed up at my house. He told me that there was going to be a Crystal Skull conference in Arizona, and many famous skulls would be there.

I contacted the venue where the event was being held and told them I was making a film about Crystal Skulls.

I told them I was interested in interviewing some of the people from the conference.

They told me to come and take a chance.

So, I came to the conference, and approached each person about an interview. During lunch breaks, I filmed many of them for my film.

I set my intention by printing my card on the computer, and Consciousness responded in amazing and unimaginable ways.

I took a chance.

Thoughts are powerful things. Everything we think, creates our reality.

As we Integrate the understanding, that our thoughts create our reality, our thoughts become tools, that lead us in the direction of our most joyful and fulfilling life.

I was amazed at how quickly Consciousness supported my idea.

The strength of the positive emotions behind our ideas, make them manifest even faster.

Do you feel great about your new idea?

Consciousness can sense your positive emotion and will support you in powerful ways.

Can you remember a time when you thought about something, and then it showed up in your life? What was that thought?

What thought would you like to think now, to take your life in a new direction?

The Ego
Rules The Mind

Chapter 4

The Battle Within

Many sacred books talk of epic battles.

The Bhagavad-gita

It seems strange that a sacred book would start with fighting, but the fighting is a struggle within us all. The fight is against our own Ego.

The Old Testament

The stories of the Old Testament begin by covering general principles, then other stories go back to fill in more details.

The Garden of Eden

The Garden of Eden is a state of mind. In this perfect place, everything we need is provided for us. We are joyful and healthy. We do not need to work because all the food we need is all around us. We do not feel shame or guilt.

In the story of the Garden of Eden in the Old Testament, we move from this perfect place into a state of doubt, shame, and dissatisfaction.

There is a part of ourselves that causes this shift.

This part of ourselves is called our "Ego". Our Ego can lead us astray.

It is important to become aware, when our Ego is running our lives.

The Serpent speaks to Eve to persuade her to give in to her desires. This Adversary lives inside all of us. This Adversary is our Ego.

The Ego sounds very logical and appeals to our left brain, logical self. The arguments the Ego presents make sense.

> "Did God really say you must not eat from any tree in the garden?"

> "We may eat fruit from all the trees in the garden, but not from the tree that is in the middle of the garden."

> "God knows that when you eat of that tree, your eyes will be open, and you will be like God, knowing good and evil."

> "When the woman saw the fruit of the tree was good for food, pleasing to the eye, and desirable for gaining wisdom, she ate it."

It all made sense. It didn't sound dangerous the way the Serpent put it. It sounded desirable.

It is so easy to be led astray by some shiny new object or person that we want.

It is easy for us to justify our poor choices.

We come up with arguments that support what we want, even though we know deep inside ourselves, that these choices are not the best choices for us.

Indecision sets in:

"Should I eat the apple, or shouldn't I eat the apple."

Doubt sets in:

"Did I do the right thing or the wrong thing by eating the apple?"

Judgement sets in:

"And God threw us out of the Garden of Eden."

The Garden of Eden is our natural state of being, where everything we need is provided for us. We are content and innocent. We have no shame or guilt.

Indecision, Doubt, Judgement, Shame, and Guilt are all constructs of the Ego.

If we let the Ego run our lives, these attributes bring us down, and prevent us from being the best person we can be.

Our Quest in Life is to subdue the Ego, from running our lives.

The Stories of the Old Testament lead us through the many paths it takes to subdue the Ego.

Cain and Abel

The story of Cain killing Abel, illustrates the Ego becoming dominant, and taking over, essentially destroying Abel, the small voice inside.

When we listen to the small voice inside, we are guided to results that lead us into Balance and Harmony.

When we are swayed by the Ego, whose logic leads us astray, we find ourselves in drama and chaos.

Cain can also be seen as the left brain, and Abel as the right brain.

As we grow older, the left brain becomes dominant. Some people are only aware of their left brain.

We are cut off from our right brain.

We spend many years learning to reconnect with our right brain.

So, Cain killing Abel also expresses this time, when the right part of our brain "dies" or is forgotten, when our Pineal Gland atrophies.

The left brain is also where the voice of the Ego resides. This is why, our Ego may become the dominant voice in our lives, at this stage.

Can you think of a time when your Ego led you to a choice you regretted?

Are you accessing your right brain now?

Story of the Flood

The story of the great flood describes a time when people let their Ego rule their lives.

Chaos and excess became so extreme, that the world needed to be destroyed and rebuilt.

In our lives, when our Ego gets so out of hand, that we lose control, and indulge in actions that may not be healthy for us, we often hit bottom.

When that happens, we need to rebuild our lives from scratch. We need to start over and take another healthier path.

In the story of the Flood, we see how we were tossed and turned in the waters, until we came back into balance.

Has there ever been a time when you hit bottom?

What happened next?

Abraham and Sarah

Abraham represents Divine Justice and Sarah represents Mercy, Divine Love or Compassion.

On the road to eliminating the Ego, we need to bring Divine Justice and Divine Love into our lives.

We need to convert human judgement into Divine Judgement, and convert human love into Divine Love or Compassion.

When we judge ourselves, and the people around us, we are listening to the Ego.

The Ego is filled with judgement and pride.

"We are better than others, or others are better than us."

In either case, we find ourselves comparing ourselves to those around us.

This creates dissatisfaction with who we are.

We find ourselves wanting what other people have.

This can lead to depression, or self-destructive behaviors.

When we focus on human love, we find ourselves constantly dissatisfied with our lives. We find fault with our partners, and we find fault with ourselves.

"Why won't he do what I want?"

"Why can't I be what he wants?"

When we move into Divine Love or Compassion, we feel Unconditional Love for everyone.

We accept people for who they are.

We accept ourselves.

Can you think of a time when you judged yourself harshly?

What did your poor self-image lead you to do?

Sodom and Gomorra

Now the Old Testament goes back into greater detail with the story of Lot. Instead of just referring to the right and left brain in general, we now enter the brain to access the deeper parts of ourselves in the Pineal Gland.

The story of Lot, Abraham's brother's son, tells the story of what happens next. The Ego has led humanity to its lowest point in Sodom and Gomorra.

By breaking out of this pattern, by exploding Sodom and Gomorra, the Pineal Gland is activated.

In our lives after we hit bottom we often find ourselves on a road to recovery.

We often seek spiritual guidance and open ourselves up to healthier ways of being.

During this process, we may change our diet, meditate, do breathing exercises, yoga, and other practices to become centered and balanced again.

As a result of these practices, our energetic bodies are activated, and we often find ourselves reconnecting to the small voice inside.

We find our Pineal Glands are working again.

Lot's Story is the story of the Pineal Gland being activated.

Lot represents the Pineal Gland.

Lot and Abraham separate.

Lot goes to Sodom and Gomorra and Abraham goes to Canaan, The Promised Land.

Sodom is the place where the senses take in information and sends this information to the Pineal Gland.

Gomorra is the place that stimulates the brain sand with the catalyst osmium, at the bottom of the Pineal Gland, causing an explosion.

The bottom of the Pineal Gland contains osmium, phosphorus, and calcium. This is called brain sand.

Lot's two daughters represent the two elements of phosphorus and calcium.

Lot's wife represents this brain sand when she is turned into a pillar of salt, after the explosion.

The energy taken in by the senses, electromagnetic energy or light, stimulates the chemicals at the bottom of the Pineal Gland causing an explosion.

This activates the Pineal Gland.

Once activated, the Pineal Gland can receive the small voice inside, and interact with higher levels of Consciousness.

The Pineal Gland shrinks during puberty.

This is like Lot going to Sodom and Gomorra, a time when humanity's ability to gain access to the small voice inside, was at its lowest point.

Through meditation and other exercises, we can move energy through our bodies to activate our Pineal Gland.

I have a Pineal Gland activation meditation that you can access on my website to accomplish this.

It is called "Reunion and Rejuvenation" in the Workshops section of www.LightFromInside.com or www.ShirleyRose.com.

Can you remember a time when you hit rock bottom?

Did you seek a spiritual path to recover?

Abraham Sacrificing Isaac

Once our Pineal Gland is activated, we are equipped to battle the Ego more effectively.

In the story of Abraham sacrificing Isaac, we see the next step toward destroying the Ego within us.

Isaac represented Abraham's Ego.

We love our Ego like a child. It is a part of ourselves.

When Abraham is willing to do God's will, over his own love for his son who represents his Ego, Abraham symbolically kills his own Ego.

When we transition from physical love to Divine Love, we enter a stage in our life that elevates us into our Higher Self.

From this new Higher Self perspective, our world, our thoughts and our actions take on new meaning.

We now see the symbolic meaning of the experiences in our lives.

Instead of getting caught up in a situation, we notice the lessons we are learning from our experience.

Instead of reacting to experiences, we are reflecting on our experiences, and Integrating revelations, that guide us in new directions.

We are Integrating all the time. We see our lessons. We understand why we bring situations into our lives to focus on.

We transform old traumas, and clear them out of our physical, emotional, mental and spiritual bodies.

We notice the steps we are taking to subdue the Ego within us.

Gradually, the voice of the Ego grows weaker, and the small voice inside grows stronger.

We find ourselves following the small voice inside more often.

And we notice that when we follow the Ego, we often encounter undesirable results.

Our insights increase as our connection to the small voice inside gets clearer.

Can you remember a time when you were sitting still, and you got a great idea?

What happened when you followed through with this idea?

Esau and Jacob

When the part of Isaac that is the Ego dies, he gains access to his Higher Self. Isaac is then transformed into his Higher Self.

When we access and merge with our Higher Self, our powers of Reason become active.

Isaac and Rebecca met and fell in love.

They had twin boys Esau and Jacob. Esau was born first, and Jacob followed.

Esau represents Nature, our Emotional Nature. Jacob represents Reason.

Although our Emotional Nature was dominant in our lives when we were young, Reason enters our life as we mature.

Reason comes second.

Reason is destined to be dominant over our emotions, if we are to continue the path of eliminating the Ego, and letting the Higher Self run our lives.

When Jacob gets the blessing of the First Born, as Isaac is dying, Reason is activated.

We see in this story, that our senses and emotions can deceive us.

When Jacob puts animal skins on his arms, Isaac is fooled into believing that Jacob is Esau, and gives Jacob the Blessing of the First Born.

Our senses and emotions can also deceive us, as we go through life.

We see someone who is beautiful and find ourselves attracted to them. This person may not be a wise choice for us, but we are swayed by what we see and what we feel.

The same may happen in business deals that are not honest. They may appeal to our greed and desire for more. Our Ego may steer us to poor choices and loss.

After we have been hurt many times, we may be ready to use Reason as a tool, to help us see more clearly.

Reason helps us to begin to suppress the thoughts of the Ego, that can dominate us, and keep us stuck in endless loops of thinking, that repeat over and over again.

Has there ever been a time when a negative thought took hold inside your head, and kept repeating over and over?

Could eating a healthy meal, or getting rest have stopped it?

Jacob and Rachel

Jacob goes on to become the leader of a great nation. But Jacob has many lessons to learn along the way.

Jacob works many years to gain Rachel for his bride. But at the last moment, Leah, Rachel's older sister is substituted for Rachel at the wedding. Jacob must work many more years before marrying Rachel.

Just as Jacob deceived his father Isaac into giving him the firstborn's blessing, Jacob was deceived by his father-in-law to marry Leah instead of Rachel.

This shows us how Karma works, an eastern term, which refers to the idea that what we do to others happens to us eventually.

If we do good deeds, many good things happen to us. If we do deceptive things, deceptive things will be done to us.

Eventually, Jacob has many wives and as a result, deals with jealousy and quarrels.

Rachel is barren for many years, and when she finally gives birth to a son, Joseph, Jacob indicates that Joseph is his favorite, causing anger and jealousy among his other children.

Jacob makes mistakes as a husband and father.

Even though Jacob is destined for greatness, he has many struggles along the way.

We find ourselves dealing with everyday struggles.

Being married, can create relationships with feelings that come up, and cause chaos and dissatisfaction.

Being parents, can cause feelings of confusion and inadequacy to surface.

So, Jacob had to deal with feelings of his own, his spouses and his children.

The struggle between emotions and Reason are ongoing.

The struggle between the Ego and Higher Self ebbs and flows, like a tide.

Lavan, Rachel's father, and Jacob argue over business with ownership of the sheep. Jacob eventually asks for all the spotted sheep, knowing there will be more of them born.

Lavan was not honest with Jacob, when he substituted Leah for Rachel. And in turn Jacob outsmarted Lavan, when he chose to keep all the spotted sheep.

Jacob felt he was justified in doing this, because Lavan would not give Jacob what was rightfully his.

Although Jacob represents Reason, his emotions led him astray many times.

Jacob wrestled with an Angel, a part of himself. His internal struggle came to a head.

There is a struggle going on inside each of us, a war for dominance. Emotions and Reason are constantly fighting with each other.

The Ego is constantly trying to take over.

We must be aware of this and pay attention to where our best interest lies.

When we are fighting with a loved one, we can stop and realize how unimportant this is. We can defuse the conflict within us, that created this situation.

By going back in time, to notice what traumatic situation in the past triggered our reaction now, we can pause a moment, before we act in the same old ways.

Jacob changes his name to Israel. In his identity as Israel, Jacob merges with his Higher Self.

Often, when we enter a new stage in life, we change our name.

The energy of this new name can create a new vibration within our being.

This higher vibration gives us access to higher realms of Consciousness.

Once these energies are activated, we can now access our higher gifts and merge with our Higher Self.

Did you ever change your name?

Did your life take a new direction?

Joseph

Joseph's story is our transitory path from the Ego to the Higher Self in more detail. This is an intermediate stage.

In the stories of Joseph, we see what can happen if we let our emotions get out of hand.

Joseph's brothers sell him into slavery. They lie to their father.

Despite their treachery, this leads Joseph to reach his highest potential. Joseph ends up in Egypt, where he becomes the right-hand man of Pharaoh and is able to help many people.

When Joseph meets his brothers again in Egypt, he teaches them a lesson, and then shows them compassion.

Joseph also represents the stage of awakening the Psychic Senses. Joseph has visions of the future and he can interpret dreams.

These gifts assist Joseph in rising to a high position in Egypt.

When our Pineal Gland is activated, we gain access to our Psychic Senses. Joseph represents the Psychic Senses.

Using our Psychic Senses is part of our path to knowing why things are happening, and what is coming next.

Our Psychic Senses are a tool that can assist us along our path.

It is important not to get stuck in the psychic senses, and to continue evolving into even higher levels of Consciousness, where we gain even deeper insights into Consciousness.

Was there ever a time when you had a vision of the past or future?

Did you ever have a dream that led you to insights?

When Joseph exhibits compassion towards his brothers, he is coming from the level of his Higher Self.

Pharaoh and the Exodus

The stories of Pharaoh summarize the many trials we go through to subdue the Ego and move to the next level of Consciousness.

Pharaoh in the Story of Exodus is the voice of our Ego, that will not let us go without a fight.

> "Let my people go. Tell Pharaoh that I will send Plagues upon him if he refuses."

Moses is the voice of the small voice inside.

Over and over again Pharaoh refuses to let the people go, and one by one the Plagues descend on him and his people.

Consciousness first sends us small warnings, like the first plagues, but if we do not listen, the warnings get larger and larger, more and more difficult to handle, until we finally give in and let go of our Ego.

If we refuse all warnings, the Plague of the death of the first-born son comes to us. We may get a life-threatening illness.

By listening, when those small early lessons come to us, we save ourselves so much suffering.

It is not easy, to let go of ideas and beliefs we have carried with us our whole lives.

During this quest, we encounter many monsters and villains that represent our fears.

In the process of letting go of the Ego, we journey to many uncomfortable places and situations, that force us to choose between the small voice inside and the Ego.

As we slay the many dragons that present themselves, we grow stronger and clearer. The small voice inside grows louder and clearer, and the voice of the Ego grows dimmer and dimmer.

We notice that each time we follow the Ego's advice, we are led to chaos, drama and grief.

When we listen to the small voice inside, Consciousness supports us and protects us.

It is a constant process of letting go of fear, surrender and trust.

Even after we let go of the Ego, it will still keep coming after us, just as Pharaoh's army came after the people, as they fled through the water of the Red Sea.

When we are consciously on our Spiritual Path, the death of the first-born son, can be the death of the Ego. It may feel like something inside us has died, and we may morn its passing.

As we choose the small voice inside more and more, leaving behind what is familiar for the unknown, becomes more comfortable.

We trust this change is leading us in the right direction.

We feel that when we follow the small voice inside, we Know we are on the right path.

Inner Knowing replaces indecision, doubt, judgement, shame, guilt and most importantly fear.

We are now free to enter the Promised Land. A place where all our needs are met, and Love and Joy are everywhere.

Inner Peace replaces discontent and we move through life with Grace.

Have you ever heard the battle in your head, going back and forth until you made a decision?

What voice did you follow? Why?

What voice would you choose today? Why?

The Five Stages

1) When we are born, we are connected to everything. We are not aware that our bodies are separate from anything around us. We are living in pure Consciousness.

When we were in the Garden of Eden we were living in this stage of infancy. Everything we needed was given to us freely. There was no struggle.

2) When we become toddlers, the idea that we are separate enters our understanding. "NO!" becomes our favorite word. We call this the terrible twos. But where does this idea of separation come from? The ideas of limitation and separation come from our Ego.

The story of Cain and Abel illustrates the beginning of sibling rivalry. We begin to want what we want without consideration of those around us.

3) Adolescence creeps in, and rebellion rules us. Our hormones send us into a roller coaster ride of emotions, up and down. We are angry at everyone and everything. We want to get away, be independent, and be alone.

In the story of the Flood, we are tossed around on an angry sea, disoriented and afraid. In adolescence, we are lost at sea searching for dry land.

4) Young Adulthood finds us in an unfamiliar world, flailing and confused. How do we take care of ourselves, find a partner, start a family? Trial and error lead us slowly, to find a way that works for us.

The trials of Abraham and Sarah, Isaac and Rebecca, Jacob and Esau, Jacob and Rachel are our trials. How do we deal with relationships, having children, dealing with our children? How do we deal with our siblings? Even when we find our true love, there are still challenges.

5) As we get older, the era of the Sage sets in. We can look back at our life and see it differently. We may notice, that we could have done things differently. Things that really bothered us before, may not have the same impact now. We mellow and gain Wisdom. Time becomes different. We are not in so much of a hurry anymore. We can take the time to slow down and enjoy, to just be.

When Joseph is born, he is his father's favorite child. He shows signs of being Psychic, interpreting dreams. He dreams of a better world. He is the part of us, that is moving into higher states of Consciousness.

Eventually, our feelings of Separation return to the Knowing, that we are connected to everything.

And so, we come full circle.

Life in its many cycles, twirls us around in a vortex spiraling upwards, towards higher levels of Consciousness.

No matter what our age, we can look inside ourselves and see what stage of development we are at. Many people remain angry rebellious teenagers into their 70s, and some people move into young adulthood at 15.

It is not our age that defines these shifts, but our state of Consciousness and awareness, that propels us to the next level.

Perhaps we are still teenagers in relationships, and Sages in our life purpose. We can be in many stages at once in different areas of our lives. Maybe we still handle money irresponsibly, but we are responsible caretakers to those we love.

We are complex beings with many parts. Each part of our lives requires attention to evolve. If we want to change a part of our lives, we can study it. We can take classes and read books about it. We can focus on what we want to be now, and let that vision lead us step by step to our ideal self.

What stage are you in?

Health

Relationships

Work

Spiritual Evolution

How The Brain Works

Chapter 5

The Right Brain

The Right Brain is where we access information that we bring back to our Left Brain.

Men and women access the Right Brain in different ways. Men access one side of their brain at a time.

There is usually a transition time needed for men to move from their Left Brain to their Right Brain.

Often the best way for them to do this is through meditation.

If men are having trouble accessing their Right Brain, they can use brain entrainment sound programs, that move their brain into alpha, theta and delta brain wave patterns.

These brain entrainment programs, can bring about balanced brain states between the Right and Left Brain.

Once experiencing where these deeper levels of Consciousness exist within them, men can often access them without assistance.

Women's brains are wired differently.

Women's Right and Left Brains are connected and sending information back and forth all the time.

Woman can learn to focus on, when they are operating from their Left Brain, and when they are operating from their Right Brain.

This only requires paying attention, and close internal observation.

During adolescence, menopause, and old age, women can also use sound brain entrainment programs to regain mental clarity and balance.

We often hear the saying "women's intuition". This comes from women's ability to tap into their Right Brain and bring back information to their Left Brain.

Children begin life with complete access to their Right Brain, and other levels of Consciousness.

Often children talk of what we label "imaginary" friends, that they describe in great detail.

Children seem to be living in other worlds at times. They are still accessing their Right Brains and moving in other levels of Consciousness.

Grownups often disregard these as fantasies, and often do not encourage them. Many children are made to feel that these experiences are childish and stupid.

How sad that we cannot nurture our children to explore these experiences with joy.

Infants and young children spend more time in the deepest Delta Brain Wave level than adults. They spend more time in REM sleep where dreaming takes place. In this way they are more connected to other levels of Consciousness.

As we age, we spend less time in Delta Brain Wave levels and less time in REM (Rapid Eye Movement) sleep, where we dream. We spend less time connected to higher levels of Consciousness.

Accessing higher levels of Consciousness is very important for personal evolution. This is where we go in meditation. This is where we can go to get answers to our questions. And this is where we go to get guidance.

What question do you have for higher levels of Consciousness?

What is the next step you need to take on your journey?

Brain Wave Levels

What we call being awake is our Beta Brain Wave Level.

The Alpha Brain Wave Level is a state between waking and sleeping. The Theta Brain Wave Level is involved in day dreaming and sleep.

The Delta Brain Wave Level is associated with the deepest levels of sleep.

Gamma brain waves are the highest frequency brain wave type, and are associated with the formation of ideas, linguistic processing, various types of learning and processing memories.

Experienced meditators have demonstrated self-induced, high-amplitude gamma oscillations during meditation.

One current theory suggests, that gamma brain waves may play a role in creating the Unity of Conscious perception and are involved in self-awareness.

The Alpha Brain Wave Level is a very creative place. We can train ourselves to go there. Often when we are falling asleep or waking up, we come up with great ideas, or solutions to problems we are seeking.

We can train ourselves to go into this Alpha Brain Wave Level state, to seek out solutions, and to find the next step we must take in a process to move forward.

One easy way to get into Alpha is to get inside our car and drive. Yes, driving puts us into a relaxed state. The motion lulls us into automatic pilot.

We do not have to think consciously,

> "put your foot on the brake and slow down."

We do it automatically, just like breathing. We do not have to think,

> "take a breath in, blow a breath out."

We do it without conscious Beta Brain Wave Level thinking.

Another way to get into the Alpha Brain Wave Level is to go for a walk.

Have you ever noticed that when you are taking a walk, ideas seem to come to you?

Another way to get into the Alpha Brain Wave Level is to take a shower.

Did you ever notice that when the water is coming down on you, flowing onto your head and body, that ideas come to you?

There are many reasons to intentionally put ourselves into an Alpha Brain Wave Level. We may be at work, trying to accomplish something we cannot seem to figure out.

By relaxing our mind, and not straining for a solution, the ideas seem to pop into our head from nowhere. This is the Alpha Brain Wave Level that goes into our Right Brain and brings information back to our Left Brain awareness.

When we are nervous about making a public speech or presentation, we can relax and put ourselves into an Alpha Brain Level state of mind.

Many people find, that the words flow freely during their presentations, without thinking of every word. There is also less heart pounding and fear seems to disappear.

This process requires trust and practice. The more we do it, the more we trust that the process will be there, when we need it.

What ideas are you looking for today?

Soften your mind, just like you can soften your visual focus, and let the ideas flow into your conscious awareness.

Theta Brain Waves give us access to our intuition and creativity.

Theta waves are connected to deep and raw emotions. Too much theta activity, may make people prone to bouts of depression and highly suggestible to suggestions, because they are in a deeply relaxed, semi-hypnotic state.

Did you ever notice that when you are watching TV late at night, that all the gadgets they are trying to sell you seem really cool? You want to buy them.

This is because you are in a semi-hypnotic state, and prone to believe what the advertisements are saying.

This is a good time to turn the TV off.

Delta Brain Waves are the slowest brain waves. They are found most often in infants and young children. As we age, we tend to produce less Delta Brian Waves.

REM (Rapid Eye Movement) sleep, where we dream, occurs in spikes from different brain wave levels.

REM cycles of about 90-120 minutes occur throughout the night. It accounts for up to 20-25% of total sleep time in adults and decreases with age. A new born baby may spend 80% of its total sleep in REM.

We can train ourselves, with practice, to be aware and observe what is going on, during these deeper Brain Wave Level states.

One way we can do this is Conscious Dreaming. We are aware of what is going on in our dreams, and can even make choices, that affect what we are dreaming. We can decide what happens, and see it happen in our dreams.

This is a very good tool, for deciding what to do in our waking Beta Brain Wave Level life. We can dream the same dream over and over, changing what we do in our dream, and observing the outcome of our choices.

When we wake up to our Beta Brain Wave Level life, we have made a choice of how to deal with a difficult situation. The outcome of our action seen in our dreams, gives us confidence that we can experience the same result in our waking state.

However, after a night of observing our dreams, we may not feel as rested and rejuvenated as we do, when we fall into unconscious states. We have been working all night, instead of resting. Solving a problem or making a difficult decision makes it worthwhile.

What will you dream about tonight?

Some people experience this as a trance state. They seem to go somewhere else outside or inside their body. They go to other states of Consciousness and have experiences. With training, we can remember these experiences.

Shamans and Healers in many cultures have trained themselves to go into Theta, Delta and Gamma Brain Wave Level states, and stay aware while they are in those states. They go into "trance", to find solutions, to find out what sickness someone is suffering from, and to know what to do to heal them.

Some Shamans and Healers have people change their names to heal them. These people essentially begin new identities and begin living as if they were different people.

This may not seem logical to a person in their Beta Brain Wave state of mind, but when speaking directly to the Subconscious, it makes perfect sense.

It may be as simple as changing the spelling of your name, using your middle name instead of your first name, a combination of your first and middle name, or it could be something completely different.

The new name holds a new vibration. When we introduce ourselves to people, we can observe their reactions. Try a few different names and see what happens.

When you find the perfect name, people's eyes will light up when you say it. People may comment on how beautiful a name that is.

You may notice that people treat you differently with your new name.

You may think of yourself in new ways too.

What is your new name?

We are receptive to words and ideas in different ways in each Brain Wave Level state.

What does not make sense on one level, makes perfect sense on another level.

We can use this knowledge to accomplish many things in our life.

When we are confused, sad, in despair, we can travel deeper and deeper inside ourselves, to the Brain Wave Level that can Integrate a deeper understanding, of why we are experiencing these emotions, and find insights that heal us.

Instead of being stuck in confusion, sadness and despair we can lift ourselves out of these states, by seeing their causes and learning the lessons these feelings have come to teach us.

We can slow down our thoughts and our breath, go into a meditative state to access deeper states of Consciousness.

This can be very helpful in finding answers.

In these deeper states, we can determine, how we can heal ourselves from physical, emotional, mental and spiritual pain.

What level of Consciousness is best for you right now?

Take a moment to go there now.

Stillness and Movement

God is Energy Standing Still.

Creation is Energy In Motion.

The Intention of Creation Is to Experience All.

When we slow down our bodies and thoughts, we come to that point of stillness. The movement of thoughts stop, and we hear the small voice inside.

We are here to have many different kinds of experience, and to learn many different kinds of lessons.

We are also here to reconnect with all levels of Consciousness and interact with these other levels of Consciousness.

Consciousness Is Connected

I once had a revelation, Integration,

> "Everything I feel, think, say and do affects everything in All of Creation."

We human beings are a point of Consciousness, that has access to every level of Consciousness, and we have a direct impact on every level of Consciousness.

Everything we feel, think, say and do sends vibrations into ALL of Consciousness and interacts with ALL levels of Consciousness.

Each emotion, thought, word and action is an energy that vibrates and moves.

These vibrations move through our physical, emotional, mental and spiritual bodies.

These energies also move through everything and everyone around us.

These vibrations ascend into higher and higher levels of Consciousness all the way to the Source.

Now we are in the fifth dimensional plane of Consciousness, and everything we feel, think, say and do materializes even faster.

I suddenly felt so empowered.

> "With great Power comes great Responsibility," as Spiderman was told.

I realized that I needed to be so vigilant in everything I felt, thought, said and did.

> "What I do makes an impact in all of reality."

> "Wow!" I was changed forever.

What would you do differently, knowing that everything you feel, think, say and do, affects everything in ALL of creation?

Everything Is Consciousness

Everything is Consciousness. Everything is self-aware. Everything has experiences on many levels.

When we activate parts of our body, we can then access the many levels of Consciousness.

Kundalini Energy is an Eastern term for an energy that exists in our Astral Bodies. Kundalini Energy is described as a sleeping Serpent, that coils around itself three and a half times at the base of our spine. This is the dormant or resting state of Kundalini.

Chakras are energy centers in our Astral Bodies. The seven major Chakras in our bodies are now transitioning into twelve Chakras, from the base of our spine to the top of our head.

When Kundalini Energy becomes active, the Serpent uncoils, and moves up through the center of our spine, and on either side of our spine, three paths on the Astral Plane.

As Kundalini Energy moves up, it activates the Chakras, described as spinning wheels or vortexes.

Kundalini usually rises in stages. It has been known to rise all at once, but this is rare. Doing deep breathing, yoga and toning, can set this process in motion.

Once activated, the Kundalini energy moves up the spine, activates the Chakras, and eventually reaches the Pineal Gland located in the center of our brain.

When the Pineal Gland is activated, we gain access to the higher states of Consciousness.

When the Red Sea parted for us, we entered the Subconscious, located in the Pineal Gland. This is where the small voice inside comes through.

The Pineal Gland

The Pineal Gland is the size of a small pea, with a tip and fatty tissue at the bottom. It produces melatonin, a hormone that affects waking and sleeping patterns.

The Pineal Gland resembles a pine cone on the outside and is often depicted as a pine cone in art and symbolism.

The Pineal Gland is larger in children than adults, and larger in women than men.

Inside the Pineal Gland are two sections of laminae, the upper and lower. The upper section divides into two strands.

Inside the Pineal Gland are follicles filled with a liquid. Inside the Pineal Gland, there is also sabulous matter made up of phosphate, carbonate of lime, phosphate of magnesium, ammonia and animal matter called brain sand.

It is proposed that the retina of the eye perceives the changes in light intensity and stimulates the Pineal Gland via the sympathetic nervous system.

The senses take in information in the form of light, which is an electromagnetic wave. These light waves are sent through the nervous system into the Pineal Gland.

Sound waves can also stimulate the Pineal Gland.

Tactile stimulation like increasing oxygen and blood flow to the Pineal Gland through inverted postures, oxygen rich chambers, and increases in atmospheric pressure, also help to activate the Pineal Gland.

Putting Frankincense Oil on the tongue can increase the functioning of the Pineal Gland.

Smelling heated essential oils or incense of Frankincense can also stimulate the Pineal Gland. Many sacred ceremonies use incense, to elevate the environment, and assist people in accessing higher states of Consciousness.

Odic forces carry the vibrations from the senses to the brain cells. Od or Odic forces are a vital energy or life force named by Baron Carl von Reichenbach.

He believed the Odic forces were responsible for Clairvoyance and Clairaudience.

The brain sand is made up of osmium, phosphorus and two forms of calcium.

Osmium is used for electrical contacts and in the chemical industry as a catalyst.

Calcium is responsible for certain communications between the brain and other parts of the body.

White phosphorus is the least stable and the most reactive, and gradually changes to red phosphorus. This transformation is accelerated by light and heat.

When there is a discharge of electricity from the light taken in from the senses, a chemical explosion takes place in the brain.

A vapor raises up from this explosion.

This penetrates the spinal cord, causing all the cells in the spinal cord to release or discharge simultaneously.

Memories are stored inside us as a permanent record through this process.

The tiny tip at the top of the Pineal Gland is an atrophied eye. We refer to this as the Third Eye where we can look into higher levels of Consciousness.

Our individual soul connects to our body by a silver cord, that is attached to the lower part of the Pineal Gland. The silver cord extends back into the higher levels of Consciousness.

In the middle part of the Pineal Gland is the Subconscious. The Conscious Mind is located in the Pituitary Gland.

There are two tiny physical channels at the bottom of the Pineal Gland, that connect the base of the Pineal Gland, with the Pituitary Gland.

Experiences from the senses are transmitted to our Subconscious, through one channel.

Along the second channel, the impulses come back, and we remember a memory.

It is important to relax the mind when trying to recall something. Trying to force a memory into our awareness does not work.

The Pineal Gland is an entry point into higher planes of Consciousness. We can reach the Plane we want by attuning our Brain Waves to the corresponding level.

The Alpha Brain Wave Level is where we access The Astral Plane.

The Theta Brain Wave Level is where we access The Divine Mind Plane

The Delta Brain Wave Level is where we access The Spiritual Plane.

The Gamma Brain Wave Level is where we merge with All That Is and become One. We no longer perceive any separation, between ourselves and everything else.

When we activate the Pineal Gland, we set in motion major changes in our lives.

We begin functioning as a part of ALL Consciousness. We start thinking holistically.

"What is best for the whole?"

We focus less on ourselves and look for ways to be of service.

Step by step, we begin serving larger and larger groups. We begin one on one, and move into small groups, then larger groups.

Everything is connected, and we become aware, that we are a part of everything.

Our Psychic Senses open. Then our Healing abilities begin. Next, we Teach our experiences to others. And finally, we start Being.

Our steady evolution leads us to take better and better care of our physical, astral (emotional), mental and spiritual bodies.

We gravitate toward cleaner diets, more positive thoughts, deliberate language, and intentional actions.

We see how our thoughts, words and deeds are working in the world around us.

What would you think, if you knew that what you thought affected everything around you?

Service to Others and Service to Self

We are told it is better to give than to receive.

I believe, it is equally important to give to others, and to give to ourselves.

It is so easy to become frustrated, when we give and give, and nothing comes back to us. We feel energetically depleted, tired and discouraged.

We begin to resent having to take care of the house, car, children, husband, pets, work, cooking, cleaning, etc.

When resentment builds inside us, it starts to fester if we ignore it. This starts the process of disease forming inside our bodies.

If we do not take the time we need to relax, rest, feed our souls, by doing the things we love to do, and have fun, then we cannot be of any use to others.

We all know the story the airlines tell us:

"Put on your mask before you assist others."

We are of no use to others if we are incapacitated from exhaustion and resentment.

Every day, we must put aside some time just for ourselves. Maybe that is five or ten minutes to close our eyes, read a magazine, or do a few body stretches to relax.

We need to do the things we love, like taking a bath, going to the movies, going dancing, and spending time with our friends.

Feeding our souls, fills up our tank of gas, so we can then serve others with an open heart. When we are joyful and energized, we give gladly.

What can you do today to feed your soul?

Training Ourselves to Listen to Our Subconscious

As we work with these new skills over and over, we can eventually bypass the negative experiences and physical pains. We can train ourselves to go inside and listen to our Subconscious directly.

By hearing the small voice inside, and following its advice, we begin to live an Intentional Life.

We can take advantage of the many opportunities that come our way.

We can connect with people who uplift us each day. We can create work that uplifts the World.

We can travel to places where we can interact with people energetically.

We can give energy to, and receive energy from the Earth, at many sacred sites around the Planet.

Our inner guidance grows louder and clearer, each time we listen and follow through on its instructions.

Even when things do not make sense to our waking awareness, after much experience with following our guidance, we learn to trust and have faith, that a higher part of ourselves, our Higher Self, knows what is best for us.

Looking for the Right Address

I was supposed to be at a meeting, but I did not have the address. People were not answering the phone, because it was a holiday. I got into my car and decided to go out to dinner.

While I was driving, the small voice inside told me to turn around and go to another restaurant. I did this. When I was seated at the restaurant, the people sitting across from me were talking about the place I needed to be. I walked over to them and asked them for the address, which they gladly gave me.

There was no way my waking awareness could have found this connection, but my Higher Self, which sees from a higher vantage point, could see how to put us together.

Life begins to be a series of synchronistic experiences. Before we were wading through muddy water with each step, now a clear path is laid out in front of us.

All we have to do is trust the small voice inside and do what the small voice inside tells us to do.

The small voice inside will never tell you to hurt yourself or others. If you hear these ideas in your head, eat a good meal, get rest, and call someone for help. This is not inner guidance.

Can you trust your inner guidance?

What is your inner guidance telling you to do today?

A Do Over

Our life experiences mirror our inner world. We bring experiences into our life to clear past traumas. We give ourselves an opportunity to redo a similar experience, and to do something different this time.

This is a tool Consciousness uses to teach us lessons.

If we are listening, paying attention, and noticing there are better ways to handle ourselves, we move through each lesson and Integrate them one by one.

By accessing our Subconscious directly, we can bypass this process, and stop re-living the same situations over and over.

We can choose to Integrate our lessons in different ways.

One way we can do this is by noticing other people in similar situations. We can shift our reactions. We can release the power these situations have over us. They no longer push our buttons.

Another way is to have a revelation or Integration inside us. We can bring back the visions of our Subconscious directly into our Conscious Mind. We can train ourselves to do this.

We can also go into other Brain Wave Levels to Integrate. This allows us to go into our Subconscious and bring back information to our waking awareness.

With practice, we notice that our outer world is reflecting our new Wisdom. We are not bringing the same old kind of experiences into our lives.

We are seeing and experiencing the world in new and different ways.

This changes everything.

We find we have more tolerance for those around us. We feel more compassion, and less judgement. We feel more peaceful and settled inside ourselves.

Our lives become a blessing that we are thankful for.

When we stop judging others, we also stop judging ourselves.

We begin loving ourselves in new ways, that bring us a deeper sense of Joy and satisfaction with All That Is.

Our world is as it is meant to be. We are no longer fighting with our ego. We appreciate every moment and know it is perfect exactly as it is.

We are now free to BE.

We no longer feel that each day is a struggle.

Activities are no longer burdens, they are simply a part of the FLOW of life.

We are at peace with ourselves.

We are at peace with Consciousness.

What insights are you having right now?

What is your inner guidance telling you to do today?

Chemical
Reactions

Chapter 6

Chemical Reactions in Our Bodies Affect Our Emotions

Chemical reactions in our bodies cause our emotions to change. When the chemicals in our body are unbalanced, it causes our emotions to be unbalanced as well.

Staying balanced requires constant monitoring. Getting our blood and urine checked by a doctor, can give us information about what we are deficient in.

Once we have this information, we can find food and supplements, that help us get back to healthy levels.

When our thinking gets fuzzy or irrational, it may be time to check these levels. There is always a reason that we are feeling out of sorts.

The chemical system in our body is the Endocrine System.

Our Endocrine System includes glands and organs, that secrete chemicals into our systems. When we look at the position of theses glands and organs, we notice they occupy the same areas as the Chakras on the Astral Plane.

Here are some symptoms you may experience when specific chemicals and Chakras are out of balance.

The 7th or Crown Chakra - Pineal Gland (regulates melatonin levels).

When out of balance:
- Depression, confusion and ridged thoughts
- Prejudice
- Fear of alienation

The 6th or Third Eye Chakra - Pituitary Gland (anterior lobe -ACTH, TSH, FSH, LH, prolactin, somatotropin, melanocyte-stimulating hormone, endorphin-peptides) (posterior lobe-stores vasopressin, oxytocin).

When out of balance:
- Headaches, blurred vision and sinus issues
- Moodiness and reject spirituality
- Unable to look at one's own fears

The 5th or Throat Chakra - Thyroid (thyroxine, triiodothyronine, calcitonin) and Parathyroid Glands (parathyroid hormone).

When out of balance:
- Thyroid, throat, TMJ, ear, neck and shoulder issues
- Communication problems, being out of control
- Fear of no power or choice

The 4th or Heart Chakra - Thymus Gland (formation of lymphocytes and antibody production) and Heart (ANF, long acting natriuretic peptide, vessel dilator, kaliuretic peptide).

When out of balance:
- Asthma, heart, lung, breast, lymphatic, back, shoulder, arm and wrist problems
- Jealousy, abandonment, anger and bitterness
- Fear of loneliness

The 3rd or Solar Plexus Chakra - Stomach (gastin), Pancreas (insulin, glucagon, somatostatin), gallbladder (Cholecystokinin CCK) and liver (IGF-1, angiotensinogen, thrombopoietin, hepcidin, betatrophin).

When out of balance:
- Digestive, stomach, pancreas, gallbladder, liver and colon issues, chronic fatigue and diabetes
- Critical, self-esteem issues
- Fear of rejection

The 2nd or Sacral Chakra - Adrenal Glands (epinephrine-adrenaline, norepinephrine, glucocorticoids-cortisone and hydrocortisone, mineralocorticoids-aldosterone) and Kidneys (erythropoietin EPO, Calcitriol, Vitamin D3, renin)

When out of balance:
- Urinary, kidney, hip, pelvic and back issues
- Commitment to relationship, ability to express emotions and have fun issues
- Fear of betrayal issues

The 1st or Root Chakra - Sexual Organs (Ovaries-estrogens, progesterone, relaxin) (Testes-testosterone)

- When out of balance: Leg, feet, immune system, arthritis, knee, sciatica and sexual organ issues
- Money, shelter and food issues
- Fear of survival

Understanding our chemical nature, and balancing these, can set us on a course for a more balanced life, with fewer highs and lows.

The happiness that most people crave is a chemical high. This chemical high cannot last forever. Western culture emphasizes this type of happiness, as the most desirable state we can be in.

Essentially, it is an addiction to being high.

Many people spend their whole lives, chasing the high of happiness. They get high through relationships, shopping, taking drugs or alcohol, eating sugar or drinking coffee.

When they come down from these chemical reactions, they feel sad.

To lead a balanced life, we need to balance our bodies. Once our bodies are in balance, we may find, that our thoughts are not so negative.

Overcoming Depression

I remember, that after my divorce I was very depressed.

I took a chance on creating a family and it did not turn out the way I hoped. I sank deeper and deeper into despair.

I found myself sleeping a lot and not wanting to get out of bed.

I also noticed, that I was not very hungry and would skip meals.

These two things: lethargy and lack of nutrition, were causing me to be out of balance.

As a result, I was thinking negative thoughts, and feeling depressed.

A friend of mine showed up, during that time, and took me away for the weekend.

I remember feeling enjoyment for the first time in a long time. I remembered, that I could be joyful without being in a relationship with a man. I had friends, children and myself.

"I was the one that made myself joyful or miserable."

I got it! I Integrated the lesson that,

"I AM responsible for my own feelings."

"Wow! What a revelation."

I was FREE.

I could find my own JOY. Joy was different from happiness. Joy was peaceful, happiness was momentarily exciting.

Can you think of a time when you were waiting for someone else to make you happy?

Can you think of a way to make yourself Joyful today?

Chemical Reactions Affect Our Thinking

I began to observe my thoughts. When negative thoughts came into my head, I decided to do something about it.

I noticed that when I ate some good healthy food, my negative thoughts disappeared.

And so, I trained myself.

If a negative thought popped into my head, I would go into the kitchen and eat an apple or a salad. Within seconds my negative thinking went away.

"This is great!"

I now had a method to use when I needed it. I had Integrated another lesson. My negative thoughts were another messenger.

"I am hungry."

My brain was saying:

"I need nourishment."

I started to read about vitamins and nutrition. Little by little I found ways to balance the chemistry in my body, by following healthy practices.

Each of our bodies is different. What works for one person may not work for another. Through trial and error, and educating ourselves, we can find the perfect combination of vitamins, minerals, food and supplements that works for us.

Like all good things in life, this takes effort. It takes discipline, and it takes the desire to be the healthiest person we can be.

Toxins in our environment also add to the fluctuation of chemicals in our bodies. It is impossible to eliminate them all, but we can do our best. Educating ourselves is always the first step.

Are we using the purest soaps, skin care products, house cleaning products, clothing detergents and dishwashing liquids?

Are we allergic to our clothes, carpet, painted walls, mattresses or furniture? Is there mold in our house?

Many of these substances can affect the hormones and other chemicals in our bodies and make us act in erratic ways.

Wouldn't it be frustrating to find out, that the reason we feel so crazy sometimes is because there are products in our environment that are changing our bodies?

Wow! Finding the answers to these things can change our lives, another Ah Ha moment, Integration.

Using fluoride free toothpaste, using skin care products without dangerous additives, eating more organically grown food and less processed food, putting filters on our showers and kitchen sink are a few of the changes we can make.

To get rid of the toxins that are already in our bodies, it is important to do a cleanse periodically. Not letting the level of toxins in our bodies get too high is very important. We can go to a doctor and have our levels checked.

It is important to see the connections, between the outside influences and the inside influences in our lives.

It works both ways.

Cleaning up our environment will also clean up our thoughts and habits.

Cleaning up our thoughts and habits will also change our environment.

So, we can approach change in our life from both directions.

When we remove clutter from our homes, we remove clutter from our thoughts. We feel more settled.

What one thing can you change in your environment today?

Changing Our Thinking Changes the
Chemicals in Our Bodies

Changing our thoughts from negative to positive, can change the chemicals in our bodies. Loving thoughts improve the body. Self-degrading thoughts can set in motion reactions in our bodies that lead to disease.

Our bodies are changing in every moment. After one year most of the cells in our bodies are new. After seven years almost all the cells in our body are new. So, the oldest body on the planet is about seven years old.

Then why do we age and grow old?

Part of the reason is that we look around us and see other people getting older. We begin to believe that this is natural.

"All people grow old."

As a whole society, we have created a belief that people grow old.

What is interesting is that the age people are thought to be "old" is changing. As a society, we are seeing that people are living longer. More people are living to be more than 100 years old today than many years ago.

We used to believe that middle age was forty years old. Now many people in their seventies and eighties seem young and fit. Our idea of what is old is changing.

As our consciousness changes, we begin to Know, that aging is not natural.

We Integrate the realization, that toxins in our air, food and water along with our home environment are breaking down our bodies natural repair systems.

Radiation from our Sun and the effects of Gravity also cause our bodies to degenerate.

We Integrate the realization, that negative thoughts can cause us to grow old and diseased.

These Integrations lead us to healthier practices, and more vigilance in watching our thoughts.

Everything begins as a thought. Good ideas and destructive ideas. Wherever we put our focus is what we see in our outer world.

When we get up in the morning and visualize the way we want our day to go, what we want to accomplish, and see everything accomplished easily, we find our day goes more smoothly.

It seems effortless as we do everything in the right time without feeling pressured or stressed out.

We trust that everything will get done, when it needs to. We do not need to push it.

Conversely, if we wake up stressed out, worried and panicked about everything we need to do, many things seem to go wrong, and many obstacles are placed in our way to confirm our beliefs.

We have a choice in every moment, Peace or Chaos, Joy or Depression.

What one healthy choice will you make today?

What one healthy thought will you choose today?

Visualizing Ease

I was coming home from far away. I knew it was going to be a very long day. I decided to visualize each section of the trip, and imagine it going smoothly and easily.

I saw myself on the bus to the airport. I knew there would be one rest stop along the way. I saw myself finding a box to put my many items in.

Next, I saw myself at the airport. I saw myself getting on the plane and storing my many items in the overhead bin.

I saw myself enjoying the long flight home. I saw myself getting through customs easily.

I saw my friend picking me up at the airport.

I saw an easy drive from the airport to her home. I saw myself relaxed at every part of the journey.

As it turned out, everything I envisioned took place. I arrived home relaxed, not stressed.

What might have been a miserable day, turned out very pleasant. I was grateful for the tool of visualizing my reality before it happened.

Can you think of a stressful event coming up in your life?

Can you visualize it going smoothly and easily?

Chemical Reactions
Affect Our Spiritual Experience

As our consciousness rises, we desire to have the cleanest, best fit body possible. This opens the channels of communication from our bodies, to higher levels of Consciousness. Everything works together.

We may be guided to go on special diets, cleanse, or fast. Following our inner guidance, can lead us to experiences on higher and higher levels of Consciousness.

We may find ourselves guided to do yoga, or deep breathing exercises. We may be guided to meditate or sit still and listen.

Opening ourselves up to this guidance, can change the chemistry in our bodies.

Growth hormones that diminish in our bodies as we get older, can start increasing again, causing us to look younger and be younger.

Postures like standing on our head, or hanging upside down, can stimulate chemicals in our brains and activate our Pineal Gland. Inverted postures also give our organs a rest from gravity and time to regenerate.

There are pieces of exercise equipment that allow us to hang upside down, or lean back in an inverted position, and be supported as we are strapped in.

These machines may be easier than standing on our head for some people.

Putting the tip of our tongue up to the roof of our mouth and holding it there, can stimulate the Pineal Gland.

When we get enough sleep, our bodies and minds have the time to rest and regenerate.

Our experiences are processed during sleep.

Our organs and body systems also have time to heal each night. Our inner guidance will lead us to the perfect practices to follow.

If we believe that our bodies were created to regenerate, we will be led step by step through the process of regenerating our bodies. Then our bodies can work as they were designed to work.

As a society we have the power to change our reality. If we all focus on our bodies healing themselves and staying young, we will begin to see this in our outer world.

We are going to live longer lives, as our collective beliefs change, and we are already seeing this in our outer world.

Can you imagine more of us living to be over 100, over 150, over 200 and beyond?

As our beliefs shift to include longer lives, many more people will enjoy extended longevity.

Recently on the news there was the story of Clarence Lawrence Matthews Born on May 1, 1906 in Oakland, California. He died at the age of 111 on July 22, 2017 in Indian Wells, California. It was fully documented.

The title for the oldest person in America goes to Delphine Gibson of Pennsylvania, who is 113, as of 2017.

As we see people living longer, we believe we can live longer too.

Medical technology already exists to keep us living longer. Artificial organs from our own cells can be generated. Processes like methylation can be turned on or off to assist healing.

Methylation is the addition of a single carbon and three hydrogen atoms (called a methyl group) to another molecule. Demethylation is the removal of a methyl group.

These on/off switches control things like stress response, how your body makes energy from food, brain chemistry and detoxification.

Stem Cell therapy can also help our bodies repair themselves.

We can also stay healthy with loving, positive thoughts, attitudes and practices.

Do you want to live to be over 100?

What would you do with more time?

Being in the Flow and Creating

Take in Prana (Breathe in Sacred Air)

Prana moves through the Nadis (astral channels)

This activates Kundalini

Kundalini rises from the base of the spine

Kundalini activates the Chakras

This activates and balances the Endocrine System

When balanced, the Endocrine System creates youth and regeneration

Emotions become balanced

Thoughts become balanced

This activates the Electrical System, the Nervous System

Information begins to flow from the Spiritual Plane, into our conscious awareness

We hear the small voice inside in meditation

This leads us to Right Understanding and Integrations

We receive guidance

We see the symbols in our material world and interpret them correctly

We see how our feelings, thoughts, words and deeds affect ALL of Creation.

Our bodies complete the circuit of receiving guidance and sending out actions to All of Creation.

We are the link between Heaven and Earth.

Focusing on What We Want

It is one of the hardest things to discipline ourselves to focus on what we want instead of what we do not want.

So many times, we focus on our worries. We have the same thought running through our mind over and over again.

"I will never be able to get out of this situation."

By beating ourselves up, we are limiting our gift of creating what we do want in life.

Worry does not accomplish anything except causing us harm and setting in motion disease in our bodies.

Worry is a form of negative thought.

The more we focus on what we do not want, the more we draw it to us.

Worry only hurts us.

Surrendering

I owed someone some money. I did not know how to pay them back.

I decided to go inside for an answer.

A name of a friend came into my mind.

I decided to call my friend and explain my situation to him. He came up with a solution.

I sold something through him and was getting monthly payments for it.

He arranged for those payments to go to settle my debt.

"What a relief!"

There is no way I could have come up with this solution myself.

By listening to my inner guidance, what could have been a very stressful situation, was changed into the amazing feeling of lifting a burden off my shoulders.

I was so grateful!

I could have spent days, weeks, or months worrying about this.

But I chose another path.

Can you think of a time in your life, when you worried about how things would get done?

Can you now think of another way you could have handled that situation?

The 5 Yamas of Yoga – Conditions of Behavior

The 5 Yamas are one of the practices of Yoga.

Our behavior can change our lives. As we evolve, we develop attributes that allow us to behave in ways, that are uplifting to ourselves and the world around us.

When we are not acting in ways that are uplifting, we may find ourselves coming from beliefs that no longer serve us.

Below are the 5 Attributes or Yamas, that can lead us into healthy behaviors. Also listed, are the kinds of actions we might find ourselves taking, without these attributes or qualities.

Comparing our actions with the lists below, can tell us where we are now, what needs improvement, and what attributes or qualities we need to cultivate, to move in new directions.

1) Non-violence

Without these qualities:

- We are cruel, speak harsh words, give unkind looks
- We feel hostility
- We have fears of not being good enough

How to overcome these:

- Eliminate our beastly nature
- Abstain from thoughts of harming all creatures
- Develop Cosmic Love

2) Truthfulness

Without these qualities:

- We have Resentment, Envy, Anger and Indignation
- Lies pollute our conscience
- Lies infect our subconscious
- We mistrust, and suspicion steals our harmony

How to overcome these:

- Thoughts must agree with words and actions
- Abide by positive principles
- Understand the phenomenon of Illusion, Maya

3) Non-Stealing / Desire

Without these qualities:

- We are stuck in Desire, the root cause of stealing
- We hoard things
- We practice gluttony, over eating
- We cling to the past and the future
- We fear not having enough

How to overcome these:

- Live in the present moment
- Know Righteousness from unrighteousness
- Develop Moral Consciousness

4) Non-Attachment / Continence / Sexual Control

Without these qualities:

- We become possessive and jealous
- We cling to financial success
- We hide our thoughts
- We fear abandonment

How to overcome these:

- Restraint not suppression of sexual desire
- Create a deep inner life.
- Open ourselves to higher spiritual consciousness

5) Non-Covetousness / Greed

Without these qualities:

- We feel disappointment
- We feel jealous and envious
- We feel anxiety, hatred and anger
- We feel lust and depression
- We have a fear of loss

How to overcome these:

- Become free of cravings and unnecessary wants
- Become free of desire
- Let go of the Ego

The Ego cannot exist without thought.

Thoughts arise from memory.

The Ego cannot exist in the present moment.

If we observe ourselves in relationships, through our feelings, thoughts, words and actions as they are happening, we catch a glimpse of the Ego.

In that light of awareness, the Ego will vanish.

And silence will blossom.

What qualities will help you improve today?

What qualities are you ready to let go of?

Our
Electrical System

Chapter 7

Our Sacred Anatomy and Electrical System

Many of the Sacred Numbers like 1, 3, 7, 12 and 33 exist in our physical human bodies and our Astral Bodies.

Our Astral Body exists in another dimension and occupies the same space as our physical body. The aura seen around our body is a part of our Astral Body.

We are one organism, but just as God is described as the three in one, the Father, Son, and Holy Ghost. We have many parts to us as well.

Inside our brain, we have the Pineal Gland, Pituitary Gland and the Optic Chiasma (point where the Optic Nerves cross). This is our trinity.

Part of our Sacred Anatomy consists of seven (becoming twelve) major Chakras in our Astral Body. These Chakras are in the area of The Pineal Gland, Pituitary Gland, throat, heart, solar plexus, lower abdomen, and base of the spine.

The Chakras are swirling vortexes or wheels and are the catalysts of Consciousness. A Chakra blockage and imbalance in one or several of the Chakras can initiate physical, emotional, mental, or spiritual ailments.

There are twelve major pairs of cranial nerves around the Pineal Gland in our skull. There are also twelve Spiritual Centers in our Astral Body in these same areas.

The twelve Spiritual Centers allow forces to flow into the material body, to transmute and spiritualize the gross body, and what we call negativity.

Our bodies are designed to process negativity. When overloaded, we feel overwhelmed. When we balance our brains, chemicals, and electric system, we can process more negativity and avoid disease from starting in our bodies.

There are twelve major meridians. The meridians are points and channels of the Astral Body, that chi, life force energy, flows through.

There are thirty-three vertebrae in our spine, which represent the thirty-three steps we must take before reaching enlightenment.

There are Nadis, astral tubes, in our Astral Body, that Pranic currents move through.

Pranic energy is the primal energy, that flows throughout the universe.

There are thousands of Nadis in our Astral Body. There are three primary Nadis the Ida, Pingala and Sushumna.

Ida starts in the left nostril and moves down on the left side of the spine. The Pingala starts in the right nostril and moves down on the right side of the spine.

The Ida and Pingala represent the basic duality in existence, the energetic qualities of masculine and feminine.

Sushumna runs from the base of the skull down the center of the spine. Once the energies enter into Sushumna, you attain a new kind of balance, an inner balance, where whatever happens outside of you does not upset you.

From this you can see that our Physical and Astral Bodies interact with each other and Consciousness.

The Astral and Physical bodies are influenced by the food and water we ingest, how we breathe, and the exercises and meditations we do.

Other factors like toning particular notes and vowel sounds, can open up and set in motion these processes in our bodies.

Our Electrical System consists of our Nervous System. Signals in our brain and heart are sent out to parts of our body to perform functions.

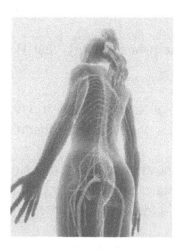

We are both Chemical and Electrical beings.

Once we have balanced our body chemistry, our Electrical bodies begin to work in better order.

Our Electrical System and Astral Body Sacred Anatomy work together.

When we take a breath, we take in oxygen and also Prana (etheric energy). This Prana travels through our body and enlivens our Sacred Anatomy.

Prana currents awaken the Kundalini Energy at the base of our spine.

The chain of events set in motion by our practices of breathing, toning, meditating, and yoga stimulate our Kundalini to rise.

This gives us a feeling of electricity running up our spine.

Our Chakras are stimulated by this energy and begin to spin in higher frequencies.

When this energy reaches the Pineal Gland inside our brain, it opens us to fuller realizations.

Our expanded vision leads us to better practices in our lives. We feel compelled to listen to the small voice inside and follow its guidance.

This starts us on a grand adventure, that creates a life of discovery and wonder.

Once setting our intention on leading our best lives, our inner guidance will lead us step by step through the practices and processes we need to do each day.

We feel like we are floating through each day effortlessly. Life becomes ease and flow.

Metamorphosis

One day in 1984 I woke up and I heard a voice inside my head. The first thing I heard was that I was my Mother's Mother in my last life. The night before, I saw the movie "Poltergeist" and was beginning to feel scared.

I stood up in the center of the room and said out load,

> "If things start flying around this room, I am going to freak out, so don't do it."

I could feel energy around me, but I did not understand what was happening to me.

I felt as though 10,000 volts of electricity were running through my body, through a column of light all around me. This lasted for weeks. At times, I felt I was losing my mind. Fortunately, I had a friend who told me she was telekinetic. She could move things with her mind.

Periodically I would call her up and ask her to say,

> "You are not crazy."

Then I would hang up the phone. Her encouragement helped me through this incredible metamorphosis. I have never been the same since.

Once my fear settled down, I began to think questions inside my head. My questions would be answered instantly as a voice inside my head.

I wanted to know everything at once. I was told that it was forbidden for me to get answers to some of my questions, because I was not ready.

I became stubborn and rebellious. I said,

> "I will not follow my guidance unless my questions are answered."

And so, I began asking every question imaginable.

> "How was the Universe formed?"

> "Why do things happen the way they do? Including Wars."

Every question was answered instantly, but I was not allowed to write the answers down. Eventually I forgot the answers. I was intoxicated by the process.

I remembered a passage in the bible that always troubled me. Moses covered his eyes when he saw the burning bush. Moses shielded himself from the light of God, because it was too bright for him to take in all at once.

I always felt that if I were given the same opportunity, I would choose to receive all knowledge instantly.

In my arrogance, Consciousness found a way to let me feel what it would be like, to be cut off from this connection. For 24 hours, I heard nothing but static. After 24 hours, I realized, that I could no longer go on living without this direct connection to Source, so I released my will and surrendered to Divine Will.

In that moment, Consciousness offered me the light. My head was filled with blazing light and electricity. It became more and more intense. It was so strong I was not sure my body would be able to withstand the intensity, and so I found myself shielding the light. Now I understood why Moses made this choice.

Wanting to understand what was happening to me, I turned to Kabbalah. I began checking out books from the library and reading them from cover to cover.

I found great comfort in the fact that the things I was hearing in my head were printed on the pages of these books.

The word pendulum indicated the concept of swinging from one extreme to the other in our everyday experiences, eventually choosing to settle in the center of moderation in all things. Just like the pendulum that eventually slows and settles in the center.

This is how we learn. We go to one extreme in our actions. When this path does not work, we go to the opposite extreme. Eventually we find that some place in the middle is a much wiser path.

Little by little, I began to understand what was happening to me. I had become Clairaudient. Clairaudience is the ability to receive messages from a higher level of Consciousness inside one's head.

A channel of energy was opened up inside me, which gave me direct access to information on every subject imaginable. I only had to think a question, for it to be instantly answered in my head.

As time went on, I could see how Consciousness prepared my body step by step, to receive more intense frequencies. I was given foundational ideas, that I built upon like a house. Each room was filled with more miraculous splendors.

This sequential approach had its purpose and wisdom. Through this process I learned patience.

I now trust Consciousness to bring me what I need in each moment.

I trust my guidance, and each time I follow it, I am led to the perfect place I need to be.

Have you ever had an internal experience?

Where did it lead you?

In addition to our Physical Body and Astral Body, we also have a Mental Body and Spiritual Body.

All these parts of ourselves work together to help us receive inspiration.

In our Spiritual Body, we receive an idea or vision.

In our Mental Body, we create a picture of what our idea looks like completed, filling in the details.

In our Astral Body, we formulate the steps we need to take, to bring our inspiration into form.

Finally, we take one step at a time, to manifest our idea in our Physical World.

We are co-creators and channels, that Consciousness uses to funnel ideas into the world of form. We take the actions, to bring these ideas into form.

During this process, we let go of more and more of our individuality, controlled by our Ego.

We release attachment to our Body, Mind, Identity, Emotions, Psychic Senses, Personality, Beliefs, Behaviors, Personal Desires, and Personal Ambitions.

All these have energies and frequencies, that interact with our physical, chemical and electrical bodies.

Our feelings and thoughts change our bodies in each moment.

Our Body

In school, we were taught to have each meal include all four food groups. We were taught a lot about the circulatory and digestives systems, but we were not taught much about the lymphatic system or the Pineal Gland.

As we enter deeper into Consciousness, we are guided to change the way we eat, breath, and exercise. Some of the things we were taught, do not match what we are guided to do. People we know may think we are strange, when we tell them we are giving up meat and cleansing our bodies.

Making these choices, gives us the responsibility, for taking care of every part of our bodies inside and out. As we open to deeper and deeper parts of ourselves, we clean out more subtle systems of our bodies. We start with what we eat. Then we clean out our organs.

We use massage and Rolfing to move blocked energies out of our skin, muscles, and tissue.

We clean and unblock our lymphatic system and learn that we must move our bodies, to keep this system flowing.

The lymphatic system has no pump and is dependent on exercise, to flow properly.

We use energy work and Reiki, to clear blockages in our auric field and subtle bodies. We use meditation to clear and rest our minds, so the small voice inside can flow freely through us.

We are relearning to listen to our inner guidance, for instructions on what to do to our bodies, as we grow in Consciousness. We trust that we know what is best for us at each stage of our development.

Our Mind

When we judge others, we judge ourselves. The qualities that annoy us most in others, are the parts of ourselves, that we bury away from view.

People around us act out what is deep inside us. We use the people around us, to communicate what our subconscious is trying to tell our conscious mind.

When we become self-aware, we begin to explore all the different parts of ourselves, including our dark side.

We learned what is right and wrong, good and bad, from parents, teachers, friends, and society.

We judge our actions and the actions of those around us, according to these values.

As we enter deeper levels of Consciousness, we realize, there is no right or wrong, good or bad.

The rules for behavior change as we travel from country to country, in man's world. What is acceptable in one country, is not acceptable in another country.

In the levels of higher Consciousness, all experiences are used to move us closer to enlightenment and are in perfect alignment with our individual plan.

Our Identity

Each of us sees ourselves as the roles we take on. We are a mother, father, sister, brother, child, secretary, boss, baker, or lawyer. We buy into these identities, and often hold on to them very tightly.

When we meet people, one of the first things they ask us is:

"What do you do?"

This establishes an identity of who we are.

Sometimes, in the case of identities such as doctors, the Ego holds on to this image, and elevates itself above others.

As we enter higher levels of Consciousness, we realize that all beings are equal.

The way we choose to express ourselves in one lifetime, does not define who we are.

Each of us has tried on the roles of worker, professional, aristocracy, and royalty. The role we are playing now is a part of our choice to have many different experiences.

Therefore, it is important not to get too attached to our present identity. For some of us, this means releasing our physical image, and opening up to the true image of our Higher Self.

Our Emotions

The emotional world exists on the Astral Plane. Some systems call this the Emotional Plane.

The Astral Plane is a place of illusions.

It is like a maze where mirrors are set up. Some of these mirrors make us look taller, and some make us look smaller. Some of these mirrors make us look heavier, and some make us look slimmer. None of these images are our true reflection.

Our emotions move us up and down, from happiness to sadness. In some cases, these feelings are very extreme, moving us back and forth like a pendulum. These highs and lows temporarily move us off balance.

As we move beyond the Astral Plane, into our Higher Self, we begin to see the temporary nature of emotions. We notice, that these transitory chemical reactions do not sustain long term feelings of well-being.

We notice, that to create a lasting feeling of true Joy, we must come into balance and master our emotions, by living in moderation.

This is the central path, that quiets the wide swings of the pendulum, to rest gently in the center, still and calm.

We do not stop feeling emotions, we are just able to tell the difference between an artificial, short-term high, and true contentment.

We let go of the addiction to the chemicals that run through our bodies.

We start looking for deeper meaning in all that we do.

When we have mastered this process, we find Joy in all things.

We no longer react to situations. We allow all the players around us to have their experience, without judgment.

We do not escalate situations, into screaming matches, and dramas.

We choose to know, that every being is on the perfect path, for their optimum growth.

All we have to do is send them love and support throughout their process.

In this way, we eliminate all feelings of negativity within ourselves.

We transform hatred into Compassion.

We transform anger into Love.

This changes the chemistry in our bodies. New chemicals enter our system that supports balance and understanding.

Our bodies become lighter and vibrate at a higher frequency.

This allows us to move past the Astral Plane, into our Higher Self, on the Divine Mind or Mental Plane.

From the viewpoint of the Higher Self, the emotional body is seen clearly. Experiences are understood as lessons, and actions are considered, not automatic reactions.

Our Psychic Senses

As our path gets clearer, we notice coincidences, based on intuition, happening all around us. We may get the urge to go somewhere. When we arrive, we find people waiting there, to give us some important piece of information we have been looking for.

We notice we are in the right place at the right time more and more often.

Occasionally we get a vision of something that will occur in the future.

As our premonitions actually happen, we find validation all around us.

We begin to trust our inner vision more and more.

We are willing to open up to these gifts and allow them to become stronger and clearer.

We begin to move past our physical senses, into our psychic senses. We open our Third Eye Pineal Gland, allowing visions to flow in. We sense things about people, that our physical senses could not convey to us.

Certain objects or places cause us to "see" inner visions, of experiences that occurred in the past or will occur in the future.

It takes time and patience to get used to these new gifts.

We can become intoxicated with these new powers. We may feel an elevated sense of self-importance and think this is the end of our journey. We may think we have arrived at the highest point our evolution can take us.

We begin to control the forces of nature like the weather. We start planting thoughts in people's minds and try to control their actions.

This is a very dangerous time in our development.

The phrase,

"A little bit of knowledge is a dangerous thing"

is an appropriate description of how we can abuse our newfound gifts?

Remember the psychic senses open on the Astral Plane. The Astral Plane is the plane of illusion. Many people get stuck in this illusion. These gifts are coming from the first opening into Consciousness, and not through the Higher Self.

Many people choose consciously, or unconsciously, not to move beyond this stage because they are caught in the illusion that they have arrived at their final destination.

If we are aware of these dangers, we can move through the opening of our psychic senses.

Knowing this is only one stage of our development, that will lead us to merging with our Higher Self.

At this point in our development, we can let go of our dependency on the physical senses, knowing that our higher senses can give us more complete information.

Our Personality

Our personalities can lead us to act in ways that get us attention. Some personalities enjoy being the center of attention, and others enjoy remaining in the background.

As we grow in consciousness, we may be asked to perform a task that does not match our personality traits.

Often, we are prepared in increments for these tasks, but occasionally we must act on blind faith.

If one of our roles will be speaking in public, we may be prepared in many ways.

Overcoming Stage Fright

As a child, I was involved in many stage performances. I danced, sang, performed plays, and played instruments in public. I had terrible stage fright, but once I got on stage I loved it.

I believe these early experiences, of being on stage, were preparing me for speaking in front of crowds later in life.

As an adult, I found myself uncomfortable speaking in public again. Those old familiar butterflies in my stomach were back.

I was attending college at the time, and one of my required classes was public speaking.

I was videotaped as a part of the class.

I remember trembling inside, when I made my presentation, but when I looked at the videotape, none of that showed. This really surprised me.

In some way, it made me feel better. I was able to relax more. People were not there to judge me. They were there to listen to what I had to say.

One of the things I learned in that class was

"Know your audience!"

Keeping in touch with my audience, has become one of my favorite parts of speaking in public.

After years of doing workshops and presentations, I truly enjoy working with people. Once I relax into it, I begin to have fun and work in creative ways.

Even though my personality prefers being in the background, I chose to listen to my inner guidance and teach.

You may find yourself in a similar situation. If you trust your inner guidance, you will be led to ways to accomplish your work.

Remember, everything happens when it is supposed to happen.

We all learn patience in the end.

We are qualified to do our work. Our inner guidance does not ask us to do things we cannot accomplish. We are unique. No one else can do the work we are sent here to do.

Knowing our Higher Self has agreed to do this work, helps us feel comfortable with the instructions our inner guidance gives us.

So, in addition to everything else we let go of, we must release attachment to our small "I" personalities and embrace our Higher Self. In this way, we overcome any limitations our personalities present.

Our Beliefs

We grow up with the beliefs that are around us. We get these beliefs from our parents, teachers, siblings, and friends. Society, and our communities, dictate many of the things we believe in.

As we grow in consciousness, we begin to question the things we have been told. We begin to see patterns in nature, that differ from the beliefs of many around us.

Our Higher Self shows us a value system, that is based on Natural Laws.

We begin to act in ways, that uplift ourselves and those around us.

We realize, we are accountable for our feelings, thoughts, words, and actions, and that everything we feel, think, say, and do affects every other level of Consciousness.

To behave in new ways, we need to let go of many of our old beliefs, that keep us from being the lights that we are.

Each social group has its own set of beliefs. These beliefs change from group to group. The values of Higher Consciousness are eternal and unchanging.

Interacting with higher levels of consciousness in full awareness, makes us accountable to a higher standard.

There are times in our lives, when we are guided to act in ways that make the people around us uncomfortable. If we send love to these people, we can ease their reactions a bit.

But we must remain true to our inner guidance.

If we detach from their reactions, it can make our journey easier.

The more experience we have with our inner guidance, the more we trust the information that comes through.

Surrendering

I was once guided to pack up my home and go to another country. When I arrived, I had no reservations and did not know where to go.

After hyperventilating, I took a few deep breaths and calmed myself. Once I relaxed I was guided each step of the way.

People met me and guided me through many sacred sites and I was given many places to stay. I had a wonderful time once I relaxed.

Sometimes, we are given information in stages. Knowing an entire plan can be overwhelming. Our inner guidance knows just how much to reveal.

Step by step, we are led to complete our tasks.

If we stay true to our inner guidance, we will always be cared for and safe.

Letting go of beliefs, that hold us back from doing our work, is vital to our evolution.

Our Behavior

Every day we create habits.

We are often unconscious of what we are doing.

Occasionally, someone around us may point out behaviors that are disruptive. At these times, we often sit down, and examine how we are acting.

We may decide certain behaviors no longer serve us. Then we choose to consciously make changes in our lives.

As we raise our consciousness, we can choose to let go of behaviors that no longer serve us.

We can create new habits, and build new behaviors, that help us act in loving, balanced ways.

Through experience, we have learned, that allowing ourselves to go to extreme behaviors, is no longer effective.

Yelling and screaming to get a point across, manipulation to get what we want, putting others down so we can feel superior, are examples of behaviors we are beginning to shift for ourselves, and the whole planet.

By finding new ways to behave, we are opening new possibilities in the Akashic Records, where our thoughts and actions are stored.

Others may find new solutions to old problems, by tapping into the Akashic Records. Eventually, the 100th monkey point will be reached, where people are acting in new ways to activate people everywhere to behave in new ways.

These patterns must start somewhere.

"If not us then who?"

Taking responsibility for our feelings, thoughts, words, and actions is an important step.

If we find ourselves having a negative thought, we need to STOP and figure out why we are out of balance. Are we hungry?

Eating something may change the chemistry in our brain enough, to change the thought to something more positive.

Eventually this will become a new pattern.

Every time we catch ourselves gossiping or criticizing, we need to STOP and say something more positive, or walk away from the conversation.

We have the awareness, that a higher part of ourselves is watching us. We must speak in ways, that uplift and inspire those around us.

Finally, we notice our actions. If we feel a situation could have been handled in a better way, we can try it next time.

We can be conscious, of what we are doing, as we are doing it.

We can act in ways that help raise our vibrations, and the vibrations of those around us. We are the light.

Each of us is moving towards the expression of our Higher Self. The more we can express our Higher Self, the more courage we give to others to do the same.

We are a link in the chain.

Every link is important and supports the one next to them.

We can be pure and clear channels of Higher Consciousness on Earth.

Our Personal Desire

Sometimes, we get caught up in an idea. It feels like our passion. There is a very subtle distinction in the pit of our stomach, that helps us know this is a personal desire.

We find ourselves really wanting this.

We try to control the outcome of our actions, moving situations into place.

When we find ourselves in this position, but we are not getting the results we want, we may want to take a second look at what is really going on.

We may "think" we are following our guidance, but if we are caught up in the result, we are being guided by our Ego.

When we are truly guided by the small voice inside, we find ourselves detached from any result.

We KNOW that everything is in perfect order and in the right place at the right time.

We do not feel obsessed, and we find we have unlimited energy to finish our task.

To the outside world, we may look driven, but we are actually flowing effortlessly in the energy. Energy is flowing throughout our bodies energizing us.

When we are being driven by the Ego, we feel a stirring in the pit of our stomach, a discomfort.

Another clue that we are on the wrong path, is that we feel frustrated if things are not going the way we want them to.

When we are following our inner guidance, we do not really care, because we are not running the show. We just do our part and allow our Higher Self, to coordinate the rest of the program.

This frees us up from any judgement.

As long as we are connected to the outcome, we need to look more closely at our motives.

This is a process that takes experience to discern. If we tap into our Higher Self and ask to know, if we are on the right path, we will hear the answers we need.

If we are ever unsure if we are motivated by personal desire or inner guidance, we can allow ourselves some time to be still and get clear.

Consciousness will never ask us to hurt another or use another person to get us what we want. If these thoughts arise in our mind, we need to get back into balance physically, emotionally, mentally and spiritually.

If we have thoughts of hurting ourselves or others, we need to get help. It may be time for a cleanse and counseling.

Inner guidance will never instruct us to hurt anyone.

Our Personal Ambition

Our Ego would like to see us in a position of power or recognition by others.

Sometimes, we aspire to fame or fortune, so that we can feel good about ourselves.

When we look for validation outside of ourselves, we are bound to be disappointed.

Outside approval brings only temporary gratification. If we need someone else to tell us we are valuable, no amount of praise will ever be enough.

If we are trying to please our father, mother, boss, spouse, siblings, or friends, we will never feel good enough.

Personal ambition is fed by a need to go above others, to be better than others. This is usually because, we do not feel good enough or as good as others.

Comparing ourselves to others, leads us to negative feelings of inferiority or superiority.

When we enter levels of Higher Consciousness, we realize each person has equal value. Each one of us has a special role to play. Each part of the puzzle is equally important. The plan needs every piece of the puzzle to be completed.

In Higher Consciousness, we prove ourselves, by following our inner guidance.

Letting go of our own ambition, helps us see, that the role we have been given has been carefully orchestrated.

Our Higher Self knows what needs to be accomplished.

By letting go of our Ego ambition, we move into a role where all the supporting players are assembled around us.

Doors open, and we sail through easily.

When we are moving towards personal ambition, we feel a struggle each step of the way. Doors slam in our face, and we are being judged.

We may find ourselves in a state of lack, always needing money. We may feel defeated and unhappy.

When we let go of personal ambition and allow ourselves to float in harmony with our inner guidance, everything is provided for us.

We always feel safe, loved, and appreciated.

We know we are valuable, and that our contributions are making the world a better place.

We are surrounded by abundance and love everywhere we are.

We are secure in our self-worth.

We are filled with contentment.

We surrender to our guidance, knowing that our guidance is infinitely clearer than our human perspective.

We trust our Higher Selves to run our lives.

We see from this higher perspective and Understand on deeper and deeper levels, the symbolic meaning of the experiences in our lives.

We Integrate in each moment.

Our lives feel different. We react differently to situations as they are occurring.

We move effortlessly through our day.

Often, we find ourselves functioning in an Alpha Brain Wave Level of Consciousness. This feels like auto pilot, where we can just sit back and enjoy the ride.

Noticing, Observing, Synchronicity, and Wonderful Outcomes become our daily experience.

Challenges are still present, but we experience them and process them differently.

Final Integration

Chapter 8

In Summary

We have journeyed to many parts of ourselves. Now we are ready to put into practice this process of constant observing, noticing, non-reacting, and clarity in each moment.

When someone is talking to you, listen.

What is your Subconscious trying to communicate to you?

Did you hear it?

Tune in deeper inside. Let your mind go soft and enter an Alpha Brain Wave Level.

Does it make more sense now?

Use every opportunity to hear what is being said to you.

The next time there is chaos around you, observe and learn, Integrate.

How is this different from your previous experiences?

Are you feeling different about what you see outside yourself now?

Everything around us is a Symbol. Everything represents something else.

We are projecting our feelings and thoughts into our surroundings. These feelings and thoughts reflect back to us using people, places, things, circumstances, and lessons.

Our Subconscious is leading us to experiences, to make us aware of our Subconscious.

Whatever is in our Subconscious, gets pushed out into our experience and mirrored back to us.

Whatever we have repressed, comes pouring out into our outer world.

We keep re-living the same things over and over until we Integrate the lessons and move on.

We can train ourselves to see the symbols in our lives and to interpret them from the point of view of our Higher Self.

Symbols All Around Us

Angry people are all around us – We are Angry.

People are withholding love from us – We do not feel deserving of love.

People are not generous to us – We do not feel deserving of abundance.

We give and give and never receive – We feel undeserving of support.

What in our childhoods or adulthood gave us these feelings, ideas, and beliefs?

Are we ready to let go of these old patterns, so our outside world can start looking like the Garden of Eden again?

What does our ideal life look like?

In the morning visualize your day the way you would like it to go.

See each task being completed easily. See yourself floating through the day effortlessly. Notice how good this feels. Feel that feeling now.

Then go about your day and notice if things went as you imagined.

In time, this becomes a habit.

Now we can move on to envisioning larger goals.

What does your perfect relationship look like? How do you feel when you are with this person? How does this person treat you?

What does your perfect home look like? How does it feel when you walk through the front door? Can you feel the floor under your feet? Can you smell the fresh flowers on the table?

What does your ideal job look like? How do your fellow workers treat you? Are you appreciated? How do you feel when you go to work each day?

Imagine achieving your spiritual goals.

How does it feel to experience contentment and compassion?

How does your healthiest body feel? See yourself inside your body, flowing through all the systems, and noticing how clean and well running each part of your body is.

Imagine your chemical system fully balanced. Imagine your electrical system stimulating your Astral Anatomy.

Imagine the clarity of the small voice inside you. Are you listening? What do you hear?

Imagine reaching your highest potential in this life. Imagine fulfilling your purpose and doing work that uplifts all levels of Consciousness.

See yourself rising up, and expanding into All That Is. You merge and become part of the whole.

How does this feel?

Imagine:

I see people blossoming like flowers and growing exponentially. I see them reaching their goals and finding their true loves. I see respect and kindness everywhere.

I feel appreciation and gratitude for all things.

People everywhere are appreciating themselves and those around them. People are telling each other; how much they love them. People are hugging and feeling loved.

I see our governments caring about all its citizens. I see politicians wanting to help the largest number of people possible. I see cooperation between all governments. I see all differences and squabbles melting away.

I see our world working together. I see a global consciousness that treats the Earth as the precious being that it is. I see clean rivers and lakes, oceans and streams.

I see clean and nutritious food on everyone's table. I see consciousness in nutrition as the norm. I see people feeling strong and energized.

I feel contentment in all things and see the people around me content with their lives. I feel competition melting away. We only need to be the best we can be in each moment.

I see communities popping up everywhere to support the elderly and orphans. I see people lending a hand to each other and giving of their time and energy. I see people feeling needed and wanted at every age.

I see the homeless coming into safe communities to assist each other with their daily needs, forming friendships, and living meaningful lives.

I see addiction as a thing of the past. There is understanding and self-love that replaces the need to medicate.

I see mental illness as a thing of the past. I see brain chemistry aligning with our electrical systems, in ways that activate our Higher Self, giving each person the guidance, they need in each moment.

I see beautiful landscapes everywhere. Flowers and trees filled with animals of every kind, living in harmony with nature.

I see jails disappearing, as each person is now in alignment with the highest way to behave in each moment. I see self-love and deserving, being so strong in each of us.

I see a world filled with wonder and Joy for every man, woman, and child.

Picturing the best we can imagine, draws these things closer to us. The more we think about our ideal world, the clearer it gets and the sooner we can experience it.

I am ready to live in a world where satisfaction, contentment, and compassion are the norm.

Are you ready to join me?

Each thought we have, changes all levels of Consciousness.

Focusing on what we do not want, brings what we do not want closer to us.

All the negative feelings, thoughts and beliefs that we focus on, create negativity in our outside world.

Making Myself Feel Better

I remember asking my brother to carry an emergency card with my phone number on it in case anything happened to him. Of course, I was doing this to make myself feel better.

In his wisdom he said,

> "If I carry this card, something bad will happen to me."

In other words, he understood, that trying to prevent negativity, by using fear, does not work. He was so wise.

How many times per day do we have negative thoughts?

Write down every negative thought you have for one day. It can be overwhelming to see how often this happens.

Then after each negative thought, write a sentence of what you would prefer to see happen.

Continue journaling daily and notice the results.

This can become a habit that can shift everything you see in your outside world.

The Movies of Our Lives

When we go to the movies, we see an image on a screen in front of us. We know that the picture does not originate on the screen, it comes from the projector behind us. We become mesmerized by the movie, we forget where it comes from, and are completely absorbed with what is in front of us.

Our lives are like this. We see what is in front of us and forget that the projector is inside of us. We are projecting our hopes and fears, love and disappointments, into our outside world.

Take a moment to get this image in your mind.

Can you see a light projecting out of your body and creating a picture in front of you?

What do you want to project this minute, this hour, this day, this week?

Integrating this Understanding into every fiber of your being, creates a shift from thinking that:

"the outside world affects me" to

"I affect the outside world."

We are the projectors of our reality in each moment.

What do you want to see in this moment?

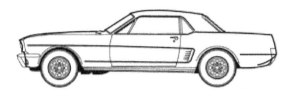

A New Car

On my son's Sixteenth Birthday I gave him a box with a note inside. It said,

"I owe you one car."

I explained to him that he could look around and find the car he wanted. I would then have a mechanic check it out, and if it was safe, I would buy it for him.

Months went by. One day he came to me and said he found it.

Together we went down to the dealer, and luckily there was a mechanic nearby, who checked the car out and gave us the okay.

The next morning when my son left for school. I told him that when he came home we would go and buy the car.

He asked me,

"How are you going to do that?"

"I don't know," I replied.

I didn't know HOW I was going to do it, only that I was going to DO IT. I made a promise I intended to keep.

I began to repeat over and over in my mind what I wanted to accomplish. The name of a friend came to me and I gave him a call and told him that I wanted to buy my son this car and did he know someone who could help me.

While we were talking he connected a friend of his in a three-way call. By the end of the conversation, his friend told me to come down to his dealership, and he would finance the car for me.

By the time my son came home, I had a check in my hand for the full price of the car. We went and bought the car together.

My clear intention and absolute faith lead me to create the outcome that I saw in my mind, in my outer world.

Every day we have countless opportunities to see wonderful things happen.

Manifesting a Man

I once took a Master Prosperity Teacher's Class, where one of our assignments was to write down a list of twelve things, that we wanted.

I started with small things like a pair of earrings and added more complicated things at the end of the list.

The first thing I noticed was how fast things were manifesting from my list. I had a hard time keeping twelve things that I wanted on my list.

Then I decided to try an experiment. I thought,

"What if I envisioned my ideal man?"

"Would this materialize too?"

And so, I began. I wrote and wrote and wrote. I decided to get as specific as I could. I chose eye color, hair color, height, and personality. I also added all the things I did not want, no smoking etc.

A few days later, the small voice inside told me to go back and take off all the things I did not want. I did this.

A short time later, this person showed up in my life. I was amazed at what we have the power to create.

Again "With Great Power comes Great Responsibility."

Be careful what you ask for.

Sometimes our Higher Self knows what is best for us. We find that things we think we want are not really what are best for us.

I have noticed this when some of the things I wanted in life did not come to me.

When I look back, I realize what I wanted was not in my best interest at the time.

I did not get those things, because something better was on its way. I didn't know something better was on its way, when I imagined my first desire.

Class President Election

I remember when I was in Junior High School and I ran for class president. I lost the election and was very disappointed.

Then I found out there was a special exchange program I wanted to participate in.

If I won the election, I would not have been able to participate in this program.

Everything worked out the way it was supposed to.

Perhaps it was personal desire, that drove me to want to be class president. My Ego thought it would be nice to have this.

But my Higher Self knew this was not the best path for me at that moment and led me in the direction of my highest path.

Dissatisfaction

Later in life, I noticed that I was going through a repeated cycle of eighteen months. Every eighteen months, I started to feel dissatisfied with my life.

I wanted to change everything in my life. I wanted a new job, new relationship, and new friends.

I finally went inside to ask, why does this keep happening?

What I realized was:

"Dissatisfaction is a catalyst for change."

Whenever I was evolving and changing, it felt uncomfortable to me.

I wanted that old familiar feeling.

"Did I really have to change again?"

After going through these cycles for a long time, I began to shift the way I felt about change.

"I'm just feeling this way because change is coming. I understand now."

"I am in transition."

For a long time, transitions made me frustrated.

I never knew what the next stage of my life would look like, and this made me anxious.

Over time, I became more familiar with the process. I noticed when it was starting and was able to relax into it.

I now choose to flow with change instead of resisting it.

I now know that I am moving up a spiral in the evolution of my consciousness.

Evolution and change are uplifting and leading me to greater insights.

When I Was Ready

As I evolved, I noticed, that new ideas would come to me.

Ideas from the small voice inside, came to me, when I was ready to know the next step to take.

If I took the time to sit still and listen, my inner guidance led me to many magical places.

Every day I set a path for myself. I set in motion a mindset that led me to greater Joy or greater chaos.

I chose in every moment.

I realized:

> "Diligence and discipline are required in each feeling, thought, word, and action."

This process got easier the more I used it.

When I noticed I was off track, I stopped, took a break, got something healthy to eat, and gently brought my thoughts to a more positive and loving place.

Eventually, I created the habit of creating joyful moments, that strung together to give me a joyful life.

We All Can

We all can support ourselves with good nutrition, clean sources of water, plenty of sleep, deep full breathing, strengthening exercises, meditation, toning, and visualizing.

The more we love ourselves and nurture ourselves, the more we can support those around us, without any resentment.

By creating a better world for ourselves, we are setting in motion powerful opportunities for others to follow.

Others can go into the Akashic Record, that holds the collective consciousness of everyone, and bring back ideas that they can use in their lives, now.

Every day is a new chance to shine.

We are all shinning stars.

Sometimes, figuring out why something is happening, does not make sense here and now.

Then, we need to go to another dimension, to make sense of it.

"Living in More Than One Dimension Consciously" is the next step.

But we'll leave that for my next book.

Let's Keep Going

Enjoy discounts on bundles of programs that include:

Reunion & Rejuvenation (a Pineal Gland activation)
The Truth About Aging
Maintenance For Optimum
Health Moving Into Happiness and
It's Not About Money (True Abundance)

www.LightFromInside.com

"LET THE LIGHT FROM INSIDE BE YOUR GUIDE."

Let us all hold a space for the light.

Let us all be the light.

Let us all spread the light.

LOVE

AND

SUPPORT

ARE

EVER

PRESENT

IN

ENDLESS

ABUNDANCE.

I AM LOVED.

I AM SUPPORTED.

I AM SAFE.

About the Author

Shirley Rose studied Genetics in her undergraduate work in college. On November 20, 2000, she received the Degree of Doctor of Metaphysics, Ms. D., from the Brotherhood of the White Temple, Inc. in Colorado.

Shirley bridges Science and Spirit, to show how they are both saying the same thing using different language. Science is beginning to prove many Metaphysical concepts.

From early childhood, Shirley had vivid dreams that took her to many different levels of Consciousness. In 1984, she experienced an opening of energy, that shot through her body, giving her a direct connection to the higher realms. She became Clairaudient.

This connection created a clear pathway to her inner guidance, that led her to travel to many sacred sites around the planet. During these travels, she sent energy into the Earth and received energy back from the Earth.

Shirley spent twelve years lecturing and teaching workshops. She also hosted a radio show where she interviewed some of the most well-respected people in the metaphysics world.

Today Shirley is writing books, that Integrate our multi-dimensional selves into full awareness. Taking responsibility for our feelings, thoughts, words, and actions empowers the many levels of Consciousness, and strengthens us all.

Bibliography

Chapter 5

Tanya Lewis, "How Men's Brains Are Wired Differently than Women's" Scientific American, Live Science, Dec. 2, 2013

Male brains have more connections within hemispheres to optimize motor skills, whereas female brains are more connected between hemispheres to combine analytical and intuitive thinking.

"5 Types of Brain Waves Frequencies: Gamma, Beta, Alpha, Theta, Delta", Mental Health Daily, April 2014

Dr. Tina Huang, "A Comprehensive Review of the Psychological Effects of Brainwave Entrainment."

Doreal, "The Pineal Eye"

Henry Gray, F.R.S., "Gray's Anatomy"

Chapter 6

Reshma Patel, "Warning Signs Your Chakras Are Out Of Balance", mbgmindfulness, Spirituality, April 21, 2014
https://www.mindbodygreen.com/0-13433/warning-signs-your-chakras-are-out-of-balance.html

Michelle Corey, "Methylation: Why It Matters For Your Immunity, Inflammation & More" April 9, 2015

Dr. Candace Pert, "Molecules of Emotion: The Science Behind Mind-Body Medicine" 1997

Pilar Gersimo, "Emotional Biochemistry"
Experience Life Magazine, Nov.– Dec. 2003
https://experiencelife.com/article/emotional-biochemistry/
Used by permission:

Back in the 1980s, a group of research scientists – including molecular biologist Candace Pert, neuroanatomist Miles Herkenham at the National Institute of Health and neuroscientist Francis Schmitt at the Massachusetts Institute of Technology, among others – began radically changing the scientific community's ideas of the way the human body works...

...they identified how emotions cause the body wide release (and take-up) of all sorts of information-carrying molecules, often in areas with no electrical neurons. These chemicals, known as ligands (most of which fall into the giant class of chemical messengers called peptides) perform a vast range of functions. They travel through our extra-cellular fluids and hook up with specific, highly selective receptors located on cells throughout the body. Once attached, they impart molecular messages that can dramatically impact our physiological functioning at the cellular and systemic levels.

Thanks to new imaging technologies, research scientists have now been able to demonstrate how thoughts and emotions cause distinct neuron-firing patterns within various parts of the brain. They can also observe how these patterns coincide with chemical releases and reactions throughout the body.

It turns out that biochemical reactions to mental and emotional stimuli – your everyday thoughts and feelings – occur not just in the brain but also, often simultaneously, in virtually every system of your body. We also now know that the brain and nerves, and the immune, endocrine and digestive systems (historically treated as totally distinct areas of medical specialty) are in fact capable of releasing and receiving many of the same peptides. Thus, all these systems are inextricably linked in a sort of secondary, chemically based nervous system, one that is intimately connected with (but not exclusively controlled by) the electrically based central nervous system with which most people are more familiar.

Swami Sivananda, "Yama & Niyama: The Path of Ethical Discipline", Yoga Magazine, Jan. 2009
http://yogamag.net/archives/2009/ajan09/y&n.shtml

ACE Study

The CDC-Kaiser Permanente Adverse Childhood Experiences (ACE) Study from 1995 to 1997 with two waves of data collection. Over 17,000 Health Maintenance Organization members from Southern California receiving physical exams completed confidential surveys regarding their childhood experiences and current health status and behaviors.

The CDC continues ongoing surveillance of ACEs by assessing the medical status of the study participants via periodic updates of morbidity and mortality data.

Adverse Childhood Experiences (ACEs) are common. Almost two-thirds of study participants reported at least one ACE, and more than one in five reported three or more ACEs.

The ACE score, a total sum of the different categories of ACEs reported by participants, is used to assess cumulative childhood stress. Study findings repeatedly reveal a graded dose-response relationship between ACEs and negative health and well-being outcomes across the life course.

As the number of ACEs increases so does the risk for the following*:

Alcoholism and alcohol abuse
Chronic obstructive pulmonary disease
Depression
Fetal death
Health-related quality of life
Illicit drug use
Heart disease

Liver disease
Poor work performance
Financial stress
Intimate partner violence
Multiple sexual partners
Sexually transmitted diseases
Smoking
Suicide attempts
Unintended pregnancies
Early initiation of smoking
Early initiation of sexual activity
Adolescent pregnancy
Risk for sexual violence
Poor academic achievement

Dose-response describes the change in an outcome (e.g., alcoholism) associated with differing levels of exposure (or doses) to a stressor (e.g. ACEs). A graded dose-response means that as the dose of the stressor increases the intensity of the outcome also increases.

Take the ACE Childhood Trauma Test at:

http://www.acestudy.org/the-ace-score.html

Chapter 7

Kirtanman, "Dan Brown, The Lost Symbol, 33 Little Steps to Enlightenment", Demystifind, Finding, Using & Sharing The Keys To Infinite Freedom, Oct. 11, 2009

http://kirtanmantra.blogspot.com/2009/10/dan-brown-lost-symbol-33-little-steps.html

CPSIA information can be obtained
at www.ICGtesting.com
Printed in the USA
FSHW022125271219
65089FS